a t
Tipperary Lakeside

from Nenagh to Ballina-Killaloe
and
from Nenagh to Portumna
by the River Shannon's Lough Derg scenic routes

Nancy Murphy

published by

Relay

Published in 1997
by RELAY Books
Tyone, Nenagh, Co. Tipperary, Ireland
Tel: (067) 31734

The book is published
with the support of Tipperary Leader Group

ISBN 0 946327 21 1

British Library Cataloguing-in-Publication Data
A catalogue record for this book
is available from the British Library.

Design and typesetting: RELAY
Typeface: Times, 11pt on 12 pt leading
Page size: 210 x 148 mm

Hill Profiles: Gail Connolly
Photographs: The late Very Rev. Seán Ó hÓgáin, front cover, p. 13; Mark Grace, p. 41 lower; Donal A. Murphy
Maps: reproduced by kind permission of the Government

Printed by Nenagh Guardian Ltd on 90g art

Contents

Preface iv

A Profile of Nenagh 1

Starting from Banba Square 4

To Ballina-Killaloe 6

Right for Dromineer 11

An Muileann Uisce 16

Nipping Down to Youghal Quay 18

The Garrykennedy Diversion 23

To the Graves of the Leinstermen 29

Graveyard, Lakeside Park, and Woods 30

Ballina-Killaloe: Heritage Town 37

To Portumna
– Via St. Joseph's Park 51
– Via the Streets 53

Hugging the Shore by Luska and Skehanagh 64

The Two Quays: Two Short Detours 69

To Lorrha's Famed Monastic Walls 77

Portumna where the West begins 80

Back by Borrisokane 82

Index 87

Tiobraid Árann ag Faire 90

Marketing Tipperary Lakeside 92

Preface

This is a loving evocation of the charms of an area which can hold its own for attractions of the tranquil kind. A travel writer is quoted on page 92 as identifying 'special qualities' here: 'hospitality, history and happenings'.

The book is written to be read during or after or even before a visit to any spot along the routes or detours. The scenes and their stories are viewed through the eyes of a traveller whether by car or cycle or on foot.

We go along the main scenic routes by Tipperary's Lough Derg shore, starting in Nenagh and heading first for Ballina-Killaloe and, secondly, for Portumna. There are worthwhile diversions to delightful spots signposted in the Contents.

The book is clearly keen to create an interest in lesser known features, all of course subject to change in the future as they have been in the past. It highlights the depth and breadth of amenities which, together with a wealth of accommodation, make the area a joy for tourists from abroad and for Irish residents on day, week-end or longer trips.

The local whose curiosity about one's own area is aroused will appreciate the attention drawn to features such as the flora of the area and the multiple snippets of information in a wealth of gossipy history: yesterday's happenings.

Hitherto shadowy buildings emerge with virtual personality traits; their builders and former residents are fondly recalled. There is an historical empathy with a brigadier of the Irish Republican Army, a major-general of the British Army, and a lieutenant-commander of the Royal Navy who was awarded a Victoria Cross. One meets native chiefs and colonist soldiers, sporting heroes, bishops, writers, a world-famous film director of the silent era and two equally famous film actors of today whose roots are here, a recipient of the Lenin Peace Prize, a politician and a fashion designer both known to Europe, and many a one whose mark was made deep in his or her own locality.

Go n-éirí na boíthre leis an taistealí.

Nancy Murphy, Tyone, Nenagh, is the author of *Walkabout Nenagh* (1994), co-author of the Bord Fáilte *Tipperary Guide* (1981), writer of the profile of Thomas MacDonagh in *Literature in Ireland: Studies Irish and Anglo-Irish* (1996), and consulting genealogist to Tipperary North Family History Research Centre. She has been a founder member of the Ormond Historical Society and of Nenagh District Heritage Society.

A Profile of Nenagh

The town of Nenagh is the take-off point for these two tours along the Tipperary shoreline of the River Shannon's largest lake, Lough Derg (not to be confused with the penitential island of the same name which lies in Co. Donegal). Nenagh is situated almost in the geographical centre of North Tipperary.

The name 'Nenagh' is derived from two Gaelic or Irish words: 'an' meaning 'the', and 'aenagh', fair. The first 'a' is dropped in each word, thus giving the anglicised form of 'Nenagh'. The addition of 'Urmhumhan' gives the aenegh or aonach (the modern spelling) a territorial location – the Fair of Ormond/ East Munster. Many established residents affectionately pronounce it 'Naina' which is closer to the old Irish name than the refined 'Neena'.

Nenagh town commenced as a Norman foundation, grew as a market place for a fruitful agricultural hinterland, became both a garrison town and new county administrative capital, and developed an industrial arm over the second half of the twentieth century.

Norman Foundation

As a walled town Nenagh dates from the building in the thirteenth century of a stone castle by a Norman named Theobald fitzWalter.

The first group of invading Normans had arrived in Ireland in May 1169. Later that year they were joined by other knights and followers and in August 1170 by the earl of Pembroke (Strongbow) who captured most of Leinster. In the succeeding years Norman colonies were established on conquered territory and fortified buildings erected, but much of Ireland still remained in Irish hands, including Ormond, territory of the O'Kennedys.

King Henry II of England appointed his youngest son John as Lord of Ireland. John came to view his acquisition in 1185 and initiated a policy of granting lands, hitherto uncolonised, to members of his entourage. Almost all of the area now comprising the administrative county called Tipperary North Riding – which includes the baronies of Upper and Lower Ormond – was part of the grant made by John to Theobald, eldest son of Hervey Walter of Lancashire, England.

Theobald was subsequently appointed Pincerna Hiberniae or Chief Butler of Ireland. By about 1250 title and surname had become Le Botiller, later anglicised to Butler. Nenagh was one of their principal seats in the northern part of County Tipperary until the fourteenth century when they moved to Gowran, County Kilkenny, and later still to the castle in Kilkenny city. However, Nenagh's castle and manor remained the property of Theobald's descendants for over 500 years.

Other Legacies

The first Theobald endowed an Augustinian religious foundation beside the Nenagh river at Tyone (*tigh Eoin/the house of St. John*), about one mile south of the castle. Substantial remains of the church and parts of the walls of some domestic buildings survive.

Apart from the castle and the remains of a Franciscan friary, also dating from the thirteenth century, the town's buildings date from the mid-1700s onwards when its sale out of Butler ownership led to the large-scale grant of leases and the subsequent growth of industries and buildings. The town's growth and development was accelerated in 1838 when the geographical county of Tipperary was divided into two ridings and Nenagh became the administrative capital of the North Riding.

Modern Profile

In the nineteenth century Nenagh was still primarily a market town providing services to a rich and fertile agricultural hinterland. Brewing, corn processing, coach building and iron works were the dominant industries. Small ones, like tailoring, dressmaking, millinery, shoemaking, carpentry, wood-turning, wheelwrighting, harnessmaking, printing, and monumental sculpting, provided considerable employment and were usually located alongside the place of residence, be that just a house or a shop with residence overhead. The advent of a purpose-built milk processing plant/creamery in 1914 added buttermaking.

The picture today is of a flourishing but not over-industrialised town, producing aluminium, stainless steel and copper holloware, road-signs, glass, healthcare products, including the world-famous Max Factor, Oil of Ulay and Maalox, electronics, farm machinery, meat products, fertilizers and animal foodstuffs, as well as butter, yogurt and dried milk from the much expanded co-operative creamery.

The fluctuation in population mirrors that of many an Irish town and the changing fortunes of the Irish economy: 1657 – 275; 1841 – 8,618; 1946 – 4,517; 1971 – 5,089; 1991 – 5,525.

There is a particularly strong community involvement, seen in over 120 voluntary organisations engaged in social services, development, culture, and recreation. Natives and 'blow-ins' have built up fine facilities including two rugby pitches, fitness centres, an indoor heated swimming pool with sauna, floodlit tennis hardcourts and an all-weather hockey pitch, hurling and soccer pitches, 18-hole golf and pitch-and-putt courses, a riding school, an all-weather running track and Ireland's only indoor tartan track. There's badminton, squash, and volleyball facilities a-plenty plus a Bridge Centre.

A Chamber of Commerce was established here in 1957. As members of the Association of Chambers of Commerce of Ireland they can avail of the services of an E. U. representative in Brussels.

St. Joseph's General Hospital provides acute medical, surgical and multiple out-patient facilities for the whole riding, while the area's senior citizens are catered for by a Day Care Centre and a residential home.

Nenagh is twinned with Tonnerre, a town in the Dijon area of France about 150 kilometres south of Paris. A spin-off effect of this is a succession of exchange visits of students and teachers. The Urban District Council also have an association, including mutual visits, with Moyle District Council which is centred on Ballycastle, Co. Antrim.

Ireland's capital, Dublin, is 102 miles/163km distant; the city of Limerick, 24m/39km; and Shannon International airport, 37.5m/60km.

Education and Heritage

Nenagh has five primary schools, including the Gaelscoil which teaches all subjects through the Irish language. The town also has a voluntary-run pre-school for handicapped children, a few privately-run pre-schools and one under the auspices of North Tipperary Social Services. Three post-primary schools cater for a total of 1,650 pupils.

Tiobraid Árann ag Labairt, an initiative of the Tipperary North Riding Vocational Educational Committee, has sparked off a wide use of Irish in business signboards.

Since 1984 visitors are able to visit the unusual octagonal building in local stone which houses Nenagh District Heritage Centre and a unique Gatehouse which accommodates the Tipperary North Family History Research Centre – both former County Gaol (prison) buildings (dealt with in some detail on the Portumna route).

Starting from Banba Square

The Courthouse, the oldest public building in Nenagh, is a good place to start your journey. It dominates Banba Square, known as Courthouse Square until 1920. In that year Nenagh Urban District Council purported to re-name all the town's streets and lanes as recommended to them by a Gaelic League-led group. In fact the Council's action in 1920 was invalid as the law prescribed that any renaming required endorsement by four-sevenths (57%) of a street's rated occupiers in a referendum. In 1965, after this irregularity was pointed out by a UDC member, the Council proceeded to hold a referendum to determine what each street should be called. In this case the name Banba was retained.

The building of the courthouse and adjacent gaol complex followed the division of County Tipperary in 1838, since it was now necessary to have first-class facilities for the twice-yearly assizes and adequate accommodation for law-breakers from the riding awaiting trial or serving sentences. Prior to the division Clonmel's courthouse and gaol served the whole county.

John B. Keane, a Dublin architect, drew the plans for both buildings and local builder John Hanly did the construction, using limestone quarried locally and sandstone from Drombane near Thurles for the courthouse Ionic pillars.

The joint administration of justice and local government by the nineteenth-century grand jury is echoed today by the presence in the building of Circuit and District court-rooms and County Council headquarters.

The railings were added in 1864 and for generations were the fixture to which sheep pens were attached on the monthly fair days until about 1959 when the town's mart, founded in 1957, became the sole selling point for cattle and sheep. Pigs continued to be sold on the streets for several years afterwards. The Square was also the location of the monthly horse fair which also faded out with the coming of mechanisation.

A companion volume, *Walkabout Nenagh* (1994), details the genesis and transformation of the Square's main features as well as potted profiles of some personalities involved – the Town Hall (1889) on the site of a turf market; Motor Taxation Office which began life as a Presbyterian church; SIPTU's county headquarters; the Ulster Bank on the site of 'Jerry's Yard'; the Garda Station which was a bank; Sheahan's, formerly the 'The Rialto' cinema; and the War of Independence memorial.

Not located in the Square itself but visible from it is St. Mary's of the

Rosary R.C. church. In Gothic style, it was designed by Walter Doolin, a Dublin architect and completed in 1896. Beside it is St. Mary's Church of Ireland church completed in 1860 to a design by Joseph Welland, a Board of First Fruits architect.

In the courthouse yard is the only surviving complete cell block of the county gaol's seven similar ones. Over the wall is the octagonal Governor's House and the gaol's Gatehouse which house Nenagh District Heritage Centre, where there is a scale model of the full original gaol complex.

Also visible as one looks around the square is the massive keep of the thirteenth-century Norman/Butler castle. Details of its architectural features and chequered history are available in *Nenagh Castle: chronology and architecture* (1993).

To Ballina-Killaloe

The twin towns of Ballina in Co. Tipperary and Killaloe in Co. Clare lie about 16 miles (25.75km) south-west of Nenagh where your journey begins. The route, aptly described on the signpost as 'Lake Drive', provides the traveller with spectacular views of Lough Derg, the largest lake on the River Shannon.

Ashe Road

The Lake Drive runs to the left as one faces the courthouse. It was called Cudville Road originally but was renamed Ashe Road in 1920 (for Co. Kerry-born Thomas Ashe, a member of the Irish Volunteers who died in August 1917 from the effects of forced feeding while on hunger strike in prison). It was cut to link Castle Street with Richmond Row which was on the mail coach route.

As elsewhere for parts of the route which overlap with the streets of Nenagh, one can find biographies of buildings and their residents in *Walkabout Nenagh* (1994) – St. Mary's Secondary School (1958); Wolfe Tone Terrace (1906) to the left; the memorial to the murdered Denis Carey, set into the stone wall on the right; the 'new' Post Office (1974) with its tribute to a central figure in Irish social life – the postman (see front flap); Boy Scouts' Hall (1936-7); the Great War memorial and departed ex-Servicemen's 'Hut' – an estimated 1,500 men from Nenagh and district fought in World War 1. Sergeant James Somers (1894-1918) from Cloughjordan, twelve miles north-east of Nenagh, was awarded the Victoria Cross in 1915 for his part in the assault on the Turkish occupation of the Gallipoli peninsula.

Personalities profiled in that booklet include Sean McDermott of 1916 fame; Edward Cuddy who built Cudville terrace, on the right as one nears the roundabout; its former residents of international and national stature respectively, Rex Ingram, pioneer film-maker, and Frank R. Maloney, a leader in the infant G(aelic) A(thletic) A(ssociation).

Richmond Row/St. Conlan's Road

Our route veers right at the roundabout where 'Lake Drive' is signposted. On the left a crop of new houses have recently sprung up in what was always called 'Mary Spain's field' and is now named Cudville Green.

The Post Chaise Companion or Travellers Directory Through Ireland (1786), described the road from Nenagh to Killaloe as a 'new one'. It is shown in *Taylor & Skinner's Maps of the Roads of Ireland,* first published in 1778 and revised in 1783.

E. H. Sheehan thought Richmond Row/Rd might have been named for a Richmond Allen whose name figures on eighteenth-century leases in connection with land in this area. On the other hand it could be just the Row or Road leading to Richmond townland on the road to Dromineer. This townland is called by its old Gaelic name, Killashallo, on a 1769 Gason gravestone in Nenagh's Barrack/Kenyon St. graveyard, and called Richmond on an 1829 stone for the same family in the same graveyard.

Charles, fifth Duke of Richmond (Surrey, England), who served with Wellington in the Peninsular Wars of 1808-14 against Napoleon, gave the name a high profile and it was subsequently imposed as a placename in many Irish towns and cities.

Whatever was the inspiration the name, Richmond Row, has faded into oblivion since St. Conlan, the patron saint of Youghalarra and Nenagh parishes, and of whom more anon, took over in 1920.

Between here and the Four Roads cross, which is both the bounds of the urban district and the turn-off point for Dromineer, one encounters a representative sample of Irish life in several facets. There is a modern industrial plant of USA origin and memories of local entrepreneurship from more simple days. There is a major sporting complex which has developed through several waves of voluntary effort. There is a mix of private and public housing. There is a block of Government offices which has had a similar incremental effect on the town as the courthouse, gaol, workhouse, and military barracks had in the 1830s and 1840s. Some notable public servants have lived in this area, as have several sportsmen of national stature.

Matt Hassett captained the Tipperary All-Ireland hurling champions of 1961 (the first final ever to be televised live) and was a member of the victorious 1962 team; he won four North Tipp titles with Toomevara – first in 1958, followed by the great hat-trick of 1960-2.

Mick Burns has a gold medal tally which includes no less than five senior All-Irelands, six National Leagues, four Oireachtas, and an inter-provincial Railway Cup, all won between 1958 and 1968, as well as a previous All-Ireland minor. That tally reflects both the breadth of competitions in our national game and the golden era of County Tipperary's involvement. His daughter's record reflects the growing attention to girls' and women's sport: Ciara Burns captained the Tipperary All-Ireland winners of 1992 and shared in national schools senior and junior camogie titles.

Athlete Liam Gleeson ranks supreme with ten pole vault and two javelin national senior titles between 1961 and 1974. He raised the Irish pole vault record from 12' 5" to 13'9 1/2" and captained Nenagh Olympic Athletic Club, U.C.D. and Ireland teams. Paul Donán Dempsey had a share in a national sprint relay record set by Nenagh Olympic A.C. in 1957. In juvenile ranks Jimmy Toohey (boxing), Paul Whelan (hurdles), and Catherine Moloney (relay) won national titles and Paul added a British Open indoor one.

The last house on the right, before the set-back line of detached bungalows, appears in a lease of 1903 as 'the dwelling house, factory, garden and premises known as South View Cottage' (Sheehan). For almost ninety years (1884-1972) Dagg's Mineral Water, Nenagh, was manufactured here. The founder, Richard Dagg (1858-1936), came from Birr where he had traded as Dillon, Dagg & Co. His son Richard John, born in Nenagh, carried on the business until he retired in 1972.

The house opposite is named 'Annfield'. The name derives from the late owner Jack Meagher's native townland in the parish of Inch near Thurles (rather than from Liverpool AFC's grounds!). It in turn was adopted as the name for the choral group who, as the Annfield Singers, have enhanced the town's cultural life with twice-yearly concerts since their foundation in 1978 by the late Mrs Sheila O'Brien who lived hereabouts.

The sixty-six houses in Cormack Drive comprise an Urban District Council scheme of 1987. It has a mixture of single-storey and two-storey dwellings geared to the needs of single persons, couples and families. The name was chosen by the residents and commemorates the brothers William and Daniel Cormack, natives of the parish of Loughmore near Templemore, who were charged in 1858 with the murder of land-agent John Ellis. They were found guilty, hanged outside the Gatehouse of the County Gaol and buried in the gaol grounds in May of that year. It was generally believed that they were innocent. In 1910, at the instigation of elderly relatives aided by a committee, their bodies were exhumed and taken back for re-burial in their native parish. The condemned cells which they occupied can be seen in the Heritage Centre.

Townlands are one of Ireland's unique features. Basically, a townland is made up of any number of fields. The name is usually (though not always) of Gaelic origin and similar ones are to be found all over the country. The basis for the name can be topographical, units of land measurement, type of settlement, or the name of an associated personage.

White Walls Road, absorbed into St. Conlan's Road as of 1920, began just past the present entrance to the off-the-road estate of privately-built houses called Belmont, and continued to the boundary of the townlands of Nenagh North (in which all the road traversed so far is located) and Gortlandroe (probably *gort leathan rua/the broad reddish field*). The boundary mark is a stream which crosses under the road between the first two houses after the entrance to Monaree estate some distance on.

In the Primary/Griffith Valuation Lists of 1850 there are seventy-four persons named as occupiers of land and/or buildings in White Walls Road. The valuation of the buildings ranged from five shillings (25p) to one pound with a majority valued at fifteen-shillings (75p). Many houses had no land. Of those that had, the extent ranged from 12 perches to 1 acre.

The beginning of the end for this settlement came when Nenagh Urban District Council 'in pursuance of the powers vested in them ... on the 3rd day of July 1935 made a clearance order ... ordering the demolition of buildings described hereunder ... ' The list included twenty houses on White Walls/St. Conlan's Road. Objections were lodged to the Clearance Order by some of the occupiers and owners and a public inquiry was held in Nenagh in October of the same year. Many White Walls residents were re-housed in the U.D.C.'s new housing estate, St. Joseph's Park, completed in 1936 (on the Portumna route).

A few of the houses, outbuildings and surrounding walls of the settlement survived up to 1995 in the midst of all the contrasting, substantial dwellings erected on each side of the road from the mid-1950s onwards.

Government Offices

On the right is the extensive office block of a section of the Revenue Commissioners which brought a welcome injection to the town of personnel and disposable income in 1992. They were joined in these custom-built offices by staff from four other government departments already in town, making a total of 270 workers in the complex. It had been Government policy for many years to 'decentralise' by locating sections of civil service departments in provincial towns. First mooted way back in 1980 the location was to be a modern much-glassed complex on the site of the former military barracks in Summerhill. A change of Government put that plan on hold and when resurrected again in the 1990s there was a re-think on location and on the design also.

A notable small industry which flourished just past the tree-lined entrance on the left, and where a new single-storey dwelling now stands, was Coonan Brothers. Their advertisement in the *Nenagh Guardian* of June 1938 proclaimed them to be: 'Coachbuilders and General Wheel Works, St. Conlan's Road (White Walls Road) ... wheel-shoeing, painting and rubbering. Every description of wheel built on the premises'.

Nearby 'Drom an Ailtigh' was the 1950s home of Ireland's present Ambassador to Canada, Paul Donán Dempsey – already referred to in the context of athletics. After the Dempseys came T. J. McGrath and family. Tom was Nenagh's Postmaster up to his death in 1982, and a former chairman of North Tipperary Vocational Education Committee for 23 years. The name of the house comes from a townland in West Cork from which Mrs Sineád Dempsey hailed. The McGraths preserve in use the name, 'White Walls Road'.

This stretch of the road could have been re-named Local Government Row, providing the residences, as it did, of John P. Flynn, first County Manager for both North and South Riding County Councils in Tipperary from 1942 to 1963; Charles D. O'Donoghue, Co. Engineer from 1952 to 1959; Thomas Brophy, County Manager from 1970 to 1977 for Tipperary North Riding after the two ridings 'de-grouped' in 1969; John McGrath, Co. Secretary from 1944 until his retirement in 1957. The stretch is also the home of Senator Michael O'Kennedy, Irish Commissioner (1981-2) in the European Union, who held Ministerial posts in Foreign Affairs, Finance, Labour, and Agriculture and Food while an elected member of Dáil Éireann between 1969 and 1992.

MacDonagh GAA Park was officially opened on 27 November 1942 by Frank McGrath, chairman of the park committee who had acquired the land and organised the laying out of a playing pitch and erection of perimeter fencing. Funds were raised locally to buy the field and North Tipperary GAA Board gave an interest-free loan for further development.

The field had already been well baptised before the official opening, having hosted hurling matches, including the North Tipperary hurling final, and sports organised by the Christian Brothers' Schools, Local Defence Force and the Red Cross.

The park was named for Commandant Thomas MacDonagh (1878-1916), the Cloughjordan-born teacher and writer who was executed after the 1916 Easter Rising. He was one of the signatories of the Proclamation of the Irish Republic, Director of Training for the Irish Volunteers. A twenty-five page profile appears in a re-publication of his major and acclaimed work, *Literature in Ireland: Studies Irish and Anglo-Irish* (1916, Relay 1996).

Development of the park has been on-going and a building programme was completed in 1989 which provided dressing rooms, a handball and racquetball alley and space suitable for indoor games like volleyball, club socials, concerts and fund-raising ventures. The new stand which seats 1,700 people was added in 1995. The park is the headquarters of Nenagh Éire Óg Hurling and Football Club. 1995 was a special year when the club won its first county senior hurling championship.

Over the years the park has been the training ground for parish-based players who wore the county hurling colours with acclaim. Those that spring to mind are Mick Burns, Seamus Bannon, Johnny McGrath, Terry Moloney, and the more recent ones, John Heffernan, Conor O'Donovan, Michael Cleary, Declan O'Meara, Kevin and Eddie Tucker.

The insertion of the somewhat unusual concrete forest by the gate is a reflection of the times – the spacious entrance sweep was becoming popular as a long-stay parking place for itinerant/traveller families.

Gortlandroe

On the right is a row of ten semi-detached dwellings of two different designs.

These were built for retired Irish members of the British services after World War I. Each house had one acre of ground; this has been deployed in some instances as a site for another dwelling or business premises. Some of the present occupants moved into the new houses with their parents in the 1920s.

As one approaches the next cross-roads, Gortlandroe Industrial Estate (1977) is on the right. Occupiers of the estate are Telecom Éireann, Procter & Gamble (who make here, among other products, Oil of Ulay and Max Factor), M. J. M. Electronics, and Tubex (Ireland) (plastics).

The roadway leads to the 'gusher' which caused great excitement when it was struck in 1977. It was subsequently connected to the town's water supply which comes from Newtown, also on this Lake Drive. While the gusher solved the water shortage problem, it introduced scale-producing lime to the system.

At the Four Roads cross the road to the left is known as the Dark Road – probably due to the overhanging branches of the unbroken line of trees which are a legacy from the demesne of the former Poe family Big House (in ruins). The Poes changed the townland name from Clonamuck (Meadow of the Pigs) to Solsboro, redolent of England. The road links this one with the Nenagh-Limerick road.

To the right are Ballycommon and Dromineer, 2 miles (3.2km) and 5 miles (8km) respectively. This would be a worthwhile diversion for a tourist, especially if staying in the Nenagh area and prepared to spend some time in Dromineer; a flavour of the atmosphere can be gauged from the photographs *on page 41.*

Right for Dromineer

The road goes firstly through the townland of Richmond, part of which lies in the urban area. The trees on the right mark the entrance to the former Gason residence – the house is gone but its fine four-column portico graces the front of the Irish Life building in George's Quay, Dublin.

Ballycommon

This placename may be derived from baile Uí Chomáin/Ó Comán's town, Ó Comán being a version of O'Hurley, pre-Cromwellian owners; or it may be baile cam abhann/the place of the river bend, which would be topographically accurate because of the loop in the Nenagh river here.

Daniel Grace in his *Portrait of a Parish: Monsea and Killodiernan* (1996), writes:

> Ballycommon developed during the nineteenth century around the old public house now known as the *Thatched Cottage*. But its growth as a village was hampered by the fact that the Catholic chapel and the

> national school were located some distance away in Carrig townland. A post office and forge were added during the late nineteenth century but very few dwelling houses were built. However, the settlement has expanded during the past few decades. New houses have been erected on all the approach roads, a fine Muintir na Tíre hall was built in 1963 … The village also has a shop and petrol pumps.

A change of ownership of the pub in the 1970s was followed by refurbishment and extensions to include a restaurant and function room.

Carrig

Carrig R.C. church, signposted a short distance on, is situated on an uphill stretch of the old road, having been by-passed when a new, lower stretch was cut in the 1840s. The church was built in 1833 by John Hanly, Nenagh, builder of courthouse, gaol and military barracks at the instigation of the parish priest, Very Rev. Joseph Downes. The ceiling was inserted in 1910. The timber pediment supported by ten Corinthian pillars behind the altar was preserved during the refurbishment which met the liturgical requirements of Vatican II, or, to use the full title, the Roman Catholic Church's Twenty-First Ecumenical Council, which was itself the first such since 'Vatican I' of 1869-70..

The church has three stained glass windows depicting the Sacred Heart, the Eucharist, and the apparition at Lourdes.

A chevron or v-shaped decorated stone, from the old church in Dromineer which you will see later on, is mounted in the grounds with explanatory text on a plaque alongside.

The old road rejoins the new line a short distance past the church. The next landmark is a sharp right turn at Cushmona cross-roads into a tree-lined stretch. The attractive building at the turn was built as a school in 1824 under the auspices of the non-denominational organisation popularly known as the Kildare Place Society. However, it lasted less than two decades as a school and has been a private residence since the 1850s.

In 1847 a soup kitchen, organised by the Nenagh Relief Committee, was located here to cook and distribute food to those affected by the Great Famine.

At the end of the avenue of trees the road swings left for the final stretch to Dromineer.

The widely-dispersed crop of mature trees indicate the presence of another Big House – in this instance, Annaghbeg which can be seen to your right. Built by Joshua Minnitt circa 1770 it stands on a height overlooking the Nenagh river. Joshua was a descendant of the Robert Minnitt who settled in the Knigh area (on the Portumna route) towards the end of the 1600s. Daniel Grace's history, already referred to, has biographies of the Gasons of Richmond and the Minnitts of Annaghbeg.

Dromineer

Dromineer as a placename is topographically exact: *druim an inbhir/the ridge of the river mouth.* The place itself is one of Lough Derg's principal developed harbours, exploits the lake with a full range of water-oriented facilities – yacht club, boat club, boat hire, and fishing. A sailing school, yacht hire, and a waterbus which provides trips up and down the lake, round out the amenities. The yacht club's annual regatta is held in August. Extensive mooring facilities have been provided through investment of public and private funds.

The harbour's first hotel was established here in 1885 to cater mainly for angling enthusiasts. It has flourished continuously since, albeit under different names – for many years as the Lough Derg Hotel, later as the Sail Inn and now, enlarged and modernised, as the Dromineer Bay Hotel. There are also self-catering cottages, a guesthouse-cum-general grocery, and a pub also offering food. All look out over the broad expanse of water with its changing moods and marvellous sunsets.

Dromineer Castle on the water's edge is a notable landmark for sailors to steer by and a favourite backdrop to water and boats for artists and photographers. Its date of construction has not been positively determined. The main part is of sixteenth-century vintage with the large quadrangular windows probably as recent as the seventeenth; it was occupied up to the late 1680s. Though not necessarily built by an O'Kennedy, members of the sept were in occupation in the mid-sixteenth century. Other names associated with it were Purcell and Cantwell.

But Dromineer was a settlement long before steam navigation and its emergence as an important port. The evidence for this stands as the remains of a small church situated on an elevated site close to the water's edge. Though part may be as old as the tenth century, its distinguishing features date from the twelfth century when it was remodelled in Celtic Romanesque style. These features include the finely-cut, round-headed east window in sandstone, and stones with chevron or v-shaped ornamentation which once formed the semi-circular west doorway. However, the fallen doorway was not reconstructed to its original state when repair work was done in the 1930s – some were actually set in at random in the west wall and some in the surrounding wall of the graveyard on the lake side.

Daniel Grace's parish history has a full chapter on the Dromineer area in general, and on the harbour's life as the 'port of Ormond'.

We pick up the main route, or Lake Drive, again at the Four Roads cross.

Past the cross-roads two old names, Clover Hill and Stoney High, have survived in use rather than the all-embracing one of Gortlandroe. The origin of Clover Hill is self-explanatory. Stoney High may simply describe the terrain or may be derived from the surname Stoney. E. H. Sheehan mentions a transaction between Richard Wills Gason and Charles Butler Stoney, Portland, Lorrha, relating to 178 acres in Gortlandroe.

Belleen

The road now enters Belleen Upper in the west end of the parish of Monsea and Killodiernan (sometimes called Puckane). This townland (*bilín/[location of] a small ancient or sacred tree*) has about 192 acres and straddles the road. There are still active farmyards in the midst of all the modern ribbon building.

Soon the road is accompanied by a gurgling little river on the left. Unnamed on modern maps, it is called the Clareen in earlier documents and is the boundary between the baronies of Lower Ormond and the more south-western Owney and Arra. The parish straddles the barony bounds, with the lesser portion (consisting of Fatheen, Gorteenakilla and Tullamore townlands) in Owney and Arra. The river heads off to join Lough Derg at Youghal Bay.

Hogan's Pass, the name of the next cross-roads is a well-known landmark. It is referred to as Muileann Uí Ógain (O'Hogan's Mill) in a mid-seventeenth-century record which also names Donogh, Daniel and Rory O'Hogan as owners of land in the area on which there was a water mill.

Prior to the 1840s travellers to Killaloe had to swing left here, then a right turn took them through Gorteenakilla and Cregane and on to Newtown. One could also go right and proceed through Monsea townland to the junction near that parish's ruined church, then left through Crannagh, Ardgregane, over the Clareen river and on to Newtown.

The building of the present mile-long, wide, straight road between Hogan's Pass and the point where the above two roads meet was begun under a famine relief public works scheme in the late 1840s. However, it was not completed until 1860 at a cost of £371 5*s*. The stretch is called the Esker Line as part of it goes through the townland of Esker (*eiscir/a ridge or line of sandy hills*). As the new road went over the Clareen river this necessitated the building of a neat stone bridge.

Newtown

At the end of the Esker line the road turns due west and enters Newtown townland and the parish of Youghalarra-Burgess. Not all of the parish's notable residents were natives of this area. One such was West Cork-born J(ohn) B(arney) O'Driscoll (1891-1961), who chose this end of the parish for his permanent home, conveniently close to his industrial interests in Nenagh and Portroe.

His principal focus was on the slate quarries above the village of Portroe which he re-opened in 1923. A decade later it was a thriving concern employing over 200 workers. He also founded the Barlite Co. (which made bakerlite domestic ware) and Tubex Ltd., both sited near the quarries. He played a major role in the founding of the Irish Aluminium Co., Nenagh, in 1935. He was a member of Tipperary (N.R.) Co. Council, North Tipperary Show Committee and numerous other boards and committees. His energetic life was brought to an untimely end in a traffic accident in 1961.

Of Newtown it could be said: Nealons for hurling and O'Briens for traditional music. Donie Nealon was one of the troika (with Michael 'Babs' Keating and Theo English) responsible for the selection and coaching of the Tipperary senior hurling team which won the All-Ireland hurling championship in 1989 – after a gap of seventeen years.

Holder of five All-Ireland senior hurling titles won with Tipperary between 1958 and 1965, and a Caltex hurling award in 1962, Donie Nealon is also a notable coach and administrator at club, provincial and national level. He took early retirement from the principalship of the parish's national school in favour of a GAA position as Munster Council Secretary. He was the parish's third Nealon teacher – his predecessors being his father and grandfather, Rody and Dan respectively.

Youghalarra townland was the birthplace of Frank McGrath (1886-1965), champion handballer and step-dancer, O/C, Tipperary No. 1 Brigade, I(rish) R(epublican) A(rmy) and Judge in the Sinn Féin courts during the War of Independence, businessman, GAA player and administrator. He won county hurling championships with the legendary Toomevara Greyhounds in 1912, 1913 and 1914. You have already met his name in relation to Nenagh's

MacDonagh Park.

A two-arched stone bridge, re-built in 1923 after its destruction in a Civil War incident, spans the Newtown river heading towards Youghal Bay. It inspired the name of the Bridge Céili Band, a trendsetter in the revival of traditional Irish music in the 1950s. O'Brien's house near the bridge was a renowned meeting place for traditional musicians.

The three O'Briens, Dinny (1887-1978), son Paddy (1923-1991), and Paddy's daughter Eileen O'Brien Minogue, are household names in the world of traditional music. Paddy and Eileen, with accordion and fiddle respectively, have captured individual and other All-Ireland titles in Fleadh Ceoil na h-Éireann.

Dinny played for years with the Ramona Dance Band, Roscrea, and, of course, with the Bridge Céili Band. Paddy played with the New York Céili Band until he returned to live in the parish in the 1950s. The Ormond Céili Band, founded by him in 1978, won three All-Ireland titles in a row, 1979-81, and again in 1984.

For years both Paddy and Eileen were to the forefront in conveying the art of the traditional musician to the young and not so young. Their talent, skill and effort have been rewarded with wins at junior and senior levels in provincial and national Fleadhanna in the céili band, individual, duet and trio sections.

For a few years prior to his death in 1991 ill-health prevented Paddy playing music, but his flair for composition continued and he composed an exceptionally wide range of jigs, reels and hornpipes – many of them now part of his past pupils' repertoire at concerts and in competition. 1992 saw the launch of a book of his compositions and a traditional music festival, Aonach Paddy O'Brien, followed by the release in 1993 of a cassette of his tunes played by Eileen and a former pupil, Willie Fogarty. The festival is now an annual affair held in mid-August in Nenagh.

Gerry O'Connor, Portroe, maestro of the banjo, was also a member of the Ormond Céili Band. Now living in Dublin and well-known on the music circuit, he made a cassette entitled *Time to Time* in 1992. This carried some of his own compositions and arrangements.

On the Nenagh edge of Newtown village a left turn and a few hundred metres brings one to an old water mill (see front flap) – Muileann Uisce, as the sign reads.

An Muileann Uisce

This three-storey early nineteenth-century building sits on an elevation of natural rock. The mill wheel, now idle, is not the original one but old nevertheless. It is about 20 feet (6m) in diameter and 3 ft 6 in (1m) wide with timber paddles in a metal frame. It has an unusual overshot water supply, diverted from the river. This is still flowing in profusion and some of it has been further diverted to power a generator which makes electricity for use in the Armitage farmyard.

The grist or corn-grinding mill was run by the Armitages for four generations. It ceased as a corn mill in the mid-1970s. Visitors are welcome.

The mill featured on television in 'Music in the Wood', made in Garrykennedy in the 1970s, and in 'Seeing and Doing' (1977), a Thames Television series for schools.

The waterworks you have of course,
And drafted from the purest source,
From Newtown's noisy, little rill
That used to feed a busy mill
That ground the farmer's yellow grain –
A sad exchange to Falvey's Lane;
Mayhap sometime it fed a still,
But now coerced by Bertie Gill,
'Tis flowing here against its will;
Decoyed from nature's pleasing plan
To cleanse the dirty works of man,
To mix the poison in your tubs,
To wash your glasses or your duds,
I wish 'twould wash you out of Stubbs,
I'm told 'tis free of mud and slime
But if you've got it, faith 'twas time.

Thus in 1893 did Sergeant Jack Keily greet the opening of the reservoir and waterworks located upstream from the mill and constructed to cater for Nenagh. Today the updated works supplies between 400,000 and 450,000 gallons daily to the urban inhabitants as well as to rural areas like Garrykennedy and Dromineer.

Nenagh's Town Hall architect, Robert P. (Bertie) Gill, C.E., designed and oversaw the scheme. R. P. Gill was twice married and a son of his second marriage is Tomás MacGiolla, Lord Mayor of Dublin 1993-4. Tomás served as T.D. 1982-92 for a Dublin constituency. He was President of The Workers' Party 1962 to 1988 through its evolution from Sinn Féin.

Waterford-born Jack Keily (1847-1905), a member of the Royal Irish Constabulary, was a prolific versifier. He served both in Nenagh and Ballina between 1887 and 1897 and left the area a wealth of topical verse, commemorating people, places and events.

Back to the main road now.

The townland of Newtown contains about 250 acres and lies on both sides of the road. The village's complement of buildings is typical of a small nineteenth-century settlement – church, school, a bar and grocery or two, post office, and a few private dwellings. It is very spread out; one passes through four townlands between the bridge and church – Newtown, Pallasbeg, Gortnaveigh, and Monroe.

Thirst can be quenched in Reidys and Barrys, while 'Reidy, Family Grocer and Post Office' and 'Barry, Grocer' also supply other necessities. Barry's hanging signboard is inspired by the fact that past and present generations have excelled at clay pigeon shooting, capturing national titles on a few occasions.

Just past the right-hand bend, on one's left and with its gable to the road, is the old national school in which Dan Nealon taught. This single-storey, two-roomed building is still in reasonably good shape.

At the far end of the village one finds signposts for Curraghbawn House (B & B) and Lake Drive at the next junction and hence the temptation to pursue another worthwhile diversion.

Nipping Down to Youghal Quay

The green area near the signposts has a limestone rock with a fiddle carved on it – sculpted by Morgan Murray, Nenagh. This memorial was erected in 1987 by the friends and admirers of traditional musician Seán Ryan who grew up in the parish. He also was influenced by the music sessions in O'Brien's. He won individual, trio, duet and céili band awards at the Feis Ceoil, Oireachtas and Fleadh Ceoil na hÉireann – including the All-Ireland senior fiddle in the latter in 1956 and 1957. He had his own céili band. He was a member of the first group of Irish musicians to tour the United States in the late 1960s.

That Lake Drive leads to Youghal Quay which was developed by regular patrons in the 1950s as a safe diving and swimming area. The annual Christmas morning swim for charity is immensely popular with participants and supporters.

On the way to the quay one passes the ruins of the parish's pre-Reformation church. Dating from about the fifteenth century, it may be a reconstructed older one. It is built of reddish-brown gritstone and measures about 73 feet (22m) long and 25 feet (7.6m) wide. The east window has carvings of an angel's head and cross. There is a human head on the south wall with the numerals 433 beside it (probably added much later and appears to be connected with St. Conlan's date of death).

The adjoining graveyard has some fine examples of carved gravestones depicting the symbols of Christ's passion – pincers, hammer, nails, flail, sponge, the hand that smote Christ, the cock that came alive in the pot or crowed to mark Peter's denial, and the towel with which Veronica wiped Christ's face.

An old handball alley stands adjacent. Youghalarra parish has a great tradition of prowess in this game. In 1911 its handballers were described in the local newspaper as 'unmatchable in North Tipperary ... and indeed in Clare, Limerick or Offaly'.

Like the road to Portumna this route also has a holy well. On the right, a short distance on from the alley and graveyard, is the entrance to St. Conlan/Coonlin's Well. The feast day or patron/pattern day is 24 July and the practice of visiting the well on that day and saying the required prayers was revived in 1975 and continues since.

This saint is also associated with Inis Cealtra/Holy Island in Lough Derg which lies across from a scenic viewing point nearer to Ballina.

The cult of holy wells is a pagan custom which was christianised by the early missionaries. Some wells are called after saints, others after aspects of pilgrimage – like the day the well was visited, Tobardomhnach or Sunday's well.

On the left, further on, are entrances to Youghal House and Youghal Lodge. The latter began life as a small fishing lodge, was upgraded to a family residence, housed a nautical school in the 1950s and now, enlarged and modernised, is an up-market holiday home. A World War I veteran, Maj.-Gen. Frederick Koe, C.B., C.M.C., lived there until his death in 1935.

At the quay you are looking into Youghal Bay which is about 2.5 miles (4km) wide and 2 miles (3.25km) from its mouth to its lower end – known locally by the Gaelic name of 'the Bun'. Otters are occasionally seen swimming in the Bun waters. Three rivers enter the lake in this area – the Clareen (called the Crannagh at this point), Newtown and Youghalarra; the first two you have already met and the third one you will meet beyond Newtown on the main road.

The names of people long-gone from this world are preserved on quays and points in the bay – Mickey Hogan's Point, Pakie's Island, Donovan's Point, Postman's Rock, and Kelly's or Turf Quay where locals unloaded turf brought in barges from up-lake Banagher and sold it by the basket to their neighbours.

In the late 1830s plans to construct a canal link between Youghal Quay and Nenagh made some headway on paper before being abandoned.

Lough Derg Way

On the road to Youghal Quay you will have noticed the brown fingerpost for the Lough Derg Way and depicting a walking man. This is a signposted walking tour whose Tipperary section begins in Ballina, climbs over Tountinna hill, passes through Garrykennedy and ends at Dromineer. A leaflet which points out the items and areas of interest is available in local Tourist Information Offices.

Back on the main road again:

Gort na bhFia

This end of the village has been enhanced by two schemes of houses: one built by the Rural Housing Organisation and the other by Tipperary (N.R.) Co. Council.

In the midst of these developments was Tommy O'Donnell's (died 1990) thatched gem – an award winner in a Bord Fáilte competition at a time when the social history and architectural value of the thatched house was not fully appreciated by those charged with the preservation of our rural heritage. Happily, in 1989 the Department of the Environment introduced a grant system to help defray the cost of thatching a dwelling like this.

The house and outbuildings contained the workmanship of Mr O'Donnell's predecessors, the Burkes, who were a family of carpenters.

On the opposite side of the road a plaque with 'Gort na bhFia', in Gaelic lettering, catches the eye. The houseowner, Thomas P. O'Keeffe, teacher and writer, Nenagh and Los Angeles, immortalised this townland name in his evocative poem 'Roots', printed in WORDSNARE No. 2 (a magazine of Nenagh arts) in 1974.

> The townland detonates to my axe.
> I'm driving whittled oak
> On Gortnaveigh – 'field of deer' in some prime;
> Upland browsing now, to coax
> Them down again, I lower the timberline.

Youghalarra Church

Youghalarra is one of the few parishes that can boast of having its three successive national schools surviving. We already met the oldest one and now you can see its 1931 successor. This has been adapted as a community centre since a bigger school, very much in harmony with the older one's design, was erected in the mid-1970s. The name of the school is inscribed on its datestone in the Irish language; the townland name, Eochaill Ara, translates to English as the yew wood of the Arra barony.

It was also one of a number of parishes which opted to retain its old cruciform church and refurbish it. It had been built in 1832 when Fr Dan

Ryan was parish priest; the 1970 renovation work was carried out under the direction of the then parish priest, Very Rev. Denis Kelly, to meet the liturgical requirements of Vatican II.

Fr Kelly (1910-91), later parish priest of Nenagh and elevated to the rank of Canon, compiled a booklet on the church and the parish to mark its rededication. In this he recorded, for posterity and local historians, the builders, architects, local committee and the financial expenditure.

The 1970 sanctuary is a memorial to an eminent native son, Michael Fogarty, Kilcoleman, whose long career as Bishop of Killaloe diocese (1904-55) was given a Papal distinction by means of a personal title, Archbishop-Bishop. The sanctuary was financed by his friends and admirers as a tribute to his memory.

Fr Dan Ryan (1791-1840) is one of seven priests commemorated by either a wall plaque inside or a gravestone outside in the grounds. Another is Most Rev. James Ryan, appointed Co.-Adjutor Bishop of Killaloe in 1870. He served in the parish, both as curate and P.P., for over forty years. You may see another memorial to him in Killaloe; his is the rare distinction of being thus commemorated in three churches – Burgess in the other half of this parish being the third.

This church is built of cream sandstone. One of the tasks undertaken in 1970 was to remove permanently the external layer of rendering and to point the original stonework.

The well-carved human head over a holy water font on the outside beside the door near the car park is obviously much older than the church. It may well have been brought from the old parish church which we met on the way to the Youghal Quay.

Monroe

Leaving schools, church and Gortnaveigh behind, the road heads off through the townland of Monroe (*móin rua/reddish bog*) The legacy of stone walls and mature trees of the former Power estate is much in evidence.

Pierce Power was the occupier of over 400 acres of land with buildings valued at £87 18*s*. in 1850. Later Powers sold out to their tenants in 1904 for twenty-one and a half years rent. The Powers of Monroe are interred in a large vault in Youghalarra graveyard which has no inscription apart from the date 1845.

The entrance to Monroe House (inhabited) has good piers and gate; the walls are capped with big sandstone slabs. The lodge, a standard feature at entrances to Big Houses and once a substantial building, is no longer inhabited.

Its neighbour, a short distance on, has a chequered history, having been a school, a Protestant church with residence overhead, and now adapted as a private residence. Good stretches of the lake are now coming into view on the right. The road to the left takes one through Ballymoylan and Pallasmore townlands and ultimately to the main Nenagh-Limerick road.

The unusual roof line of the house called 'The Old Forge' (on the right) catches the eye. The name preserves the fact that it was a practising blacksmith's forge up to the 1960s.

Duharra (*dúithche Ara/the Arra district*) Creamery has come to the end of its life as such and its future remains undecided. The Co-operative movement started in Ireland in 1898 and soon milk-processing plants or creameries sprang up around the countryside. From a locally-managed unit this one became part of the larger Nenagh Creamery Co.-Op as a milk collection point for local suppliers. In 1989 a small, but sophisticated, piece of electronic equipment was installed which, when operated by the supplier's card (similar to the bank pass), recorded the quantity and quality of the milk as it passed through the machinery within. Soon that was overtaken by refrigerated bulk storage tanks and collection at source.

The creamery here was burnt in November 1920, one of twelve in the county to suffer that fate at the hands of the Black and Tans at the height of the War of Independence.

The Black and Tans were the force of demobilised soldiers recruited by the British Government in 1920 to supplement the Royal Irish Constabulary who were the main target of the I(rish) R(epublican) A(rmy) during the war, 1919-21. Due to a shortage of the regular R.I.C. uniform the new force was issued with khaki trousers and dark green tunics. This colour combination led to their being dubbed the 'Black and Tans' after the famous Co. Limerick pack of hounds, the Scarteen Black and Tans.

The road enters a 'Community Alert' zone (a neighbourhood watch on people and property) at the next cross where narrow country roads head off to Youghal Quay (right) and Lackamore and Coumbeg (left) – the latter a scenic drive through a maze of roads and one not to be undertaken without local knowledge or a good road map.

Cloneygowney in Castletownarra

The next landmark is the bridge over the Youghalarra river in the townland of Ballycaridoge (the letters 'ge' are not pronounced). It is called the ford of Aghagaddy in the Civil Survey of 1654 and marks the boundary between the parishes of Youghalarra-Burgess and Castletownarra (Portroe). This survey, which lists land owners, townland names and fascinating topographical details, was made during the Cromwellian period to facilitate the confiscation and redistribution of Irish lands.

St. Joseph's Terrace, the scheme of seven pairs of semi-detached houses on the right, was built by Tipperary (N.R.) County Council in 1935.

We are now in the townland of Cloneygowney (*cluain an ghamhnaigh/*

the meadow of the milch cow). The two pairs of semi-detached dwellings on the right at the bend in the road began life as houses built for ex-Servicemen in 1924. The architect was a W. H. Howard and each had a cart shed and earth closet at the back.

The traditional layout of the Irish farmyard has been greatly altered in recent years with the tendency to move the farm buildings well away from the family dwelling. On the left there are two well-preserved examples of the old style within a short distance of each other. Here you see a rectangular courtyard with the dwelling and out-offices opening onto it – neither is now part of an active farm and one has been tastefully updated.

On the approach to the next cross-roads on the right is Shouldice's Hall, now redundant but once a real 'ballroom of romance' (1950s). At the cross one enters the large L-shaped townland of Garrykennedy (*garrdha Uí Chinnéide/the O'Kennedy garden or cultivated land area*).

The lakeside village of the same name is signposted to the right; it is a rewarding diversion, as might be suggested perhaps by the photographs on page 42.

The Garrykennedy Diversion

Garrykennedy village lies in Youghal Bay on Lough Derg. It has a dozen or so dwellings and attendant out-offices – none greatly altered from their original design.

This was once a thriving port for the export of slate and agricultural commodities and the import of turf, coal, spirits and Guinness. Passengers could board or disembark the steamers plying on the lake.

The late 1950s saw the end of commercial craft but now the updated and extended port is a busy place with cruisers, yachts and smaller boats a-coming and a-going. Attractions extend to sailing, cot racing, windsurfing and, of course, fishing.

Pat Lawless, Limerick, who sailed single-handed around the world in a 30 foot ketch, is a familiar figure in Garrykennedy sailing circles. He covered over 30,000 sea-miles during the three years, 1993-6.

There were mines here in the last century. They are described in the prospectus prepared for the sale of Julia Watson's property (which included Garrykennedy and the village of Portroe) in the Encumbered Estates Court in November 1857. Located on sloping ground not far from the lake and containing lead and silver, they had been worked up to 1851. Their remains are now submerged – Garrykennedy townland has about two-thirds of a mile of shoreline.

In the summer of 1845 the *Nenagh Guardian* carried quite a few advertisements about a proposed railway link between Nenagh and

Garrykennedy Quay. Shares in the proposed company were £20 each with a forecast made that 'not less than 50,000 tons of coal and slate would be carried on the line annually'. This ambitious plan, as with the Nenagh-Youghal canal project, was not realised.

The quay has excellent views for artist and photographer and a woodland lakeside walk with 'the slippery rocks' to sit on. Local residents, Mrs Peggy Geraghty and daughter Siobhán whose interests are botany and environmental archaeology respectively, have produced an illustrated leaflet on the circular walk which helps one to identify the trees there – conifers, Scots pine, Norway spruce, larch, oak, mountain ash, holly and birch.

It also lists the plants to be seen in the various seasons like sneezewort, harebell, wood sorrel and bluebells in spring, meadow sweet, flag iris, valerian and hemp agrimony in summer. Orange bracken, blackberries, and the berries of the mountain ash, abound in autumn. The leaflet is available in Nenagh District Heritage Centre.

For wildlife watchers there are mute swans, mallards (tufted ducks) and, if you're lucky, a red squirrel or two.

Uninhabited small houses on the road which runs parallel with the walk have been brought to life with window murals.

The O'Kennedy tower house (circa 1480) strategically sited on the shore, is one of thirteen such buildings to be found close to the water, or on a small island near the shoreline, between Portumna and Killaloe, some of which are now totally destroyed. Tower houses were the dwellings of substantial landowners and date generally from circa 1450 to 1600.

The village's letter-box, once red, now green, records the transition from the United Kingdom, personified by its monarch, E(dward) VII, to S(aorstát) É(ireann), the Irish Free State of 1922-37.

Irish Music

A number of the village houses have undergone major changes. For years the former Barge Inn, later re-named Dan Larkins, was the 'headquarters' of the Ormond Céili Band, founded by the late Paddy O'Brien. Dan Larkin, owner of the pub until 1996, and daughter Denise are noted traditional violin players and guested with the Scottish Fiddlers' Orchestra in the Albert Hall, London, in April 1990.

Memorial to Paddy O'Brien in Garrykennedy graveyard

The new owners raised the level of the old dwelling to two-storey and used thatch rather than slate for the roof. The new building preserves some emphasis on traditional music while nearby Ryans continues to be the mecca for fishermen. The renovations to that business include the addition of a beer garden.

You should return now to the signpost on the main road.

Slate

Tubex Ltd., the industry founded by J. B. O'Driscoll but now German-owned, is in the heart of slate country. Slate was created in the Silurian age, between 420 and 450 million years ago. It is formed from soft shale and clay hardened by extreme heat and pressure within the earth.

Slate has been quarried in this area since the mid-1700s. The boom years were during the 1840s-90s with high production and employment. The turn of the century saw a decline in production with the quarries going out of business in 1918.

As already mentioned vis-a-vis Newtown, the closed quarries were purchased by J. B. O'Driscoll in 1923 and brought back to successful production. Tubex Ltd., which pioneered the manufacture of collapsible metal tubes in Ireland, was opened beside the quarry by O'Driscoll in 1938. His Killaloe Slate Quarry Co. Ltd. ceased production in 1956 but some former employees continued to produce slates privately up to 1960.

The ruins of dwelling houses and out-buildings scattered around the area show that, apart from timber, the only material used in their construction was slate – for walls, door and window lintels, roofs, garden walls and gate piers.

The old quarry in Killoran townland was re-opened in 1991 by a company called Irish Slate Quarries (Killoran) Ltd. However, it closed again in 1994.

It is interesting to note that the name of the townland in which the slate is located was incorporated into the name of the production company. Previous companies favoured the name of the town of Killaloe – already known internationally as a steamer terminus and for its fishing – as part of the company name and/or the address, although Killaloe is located on the west bank of the River Shannon and so in Co. Clare. Accordingly, the slates became known as 'Killaloes'.

Portroe Village

Port rua/an elevation of reddish land. At its highest point Portroe village is about 605 feet (181.5m) above sea level. It commands a marvellous view of lake and countryside. The exteriors of most of its buildings have been replastered but one or two still display sand and lime finishes and small windows.

The centre of community activities is the Muintir na Tíre hall built by the parish branch of that organisation, 1959-60. Muintir na Tíre (= people of the countryside) is the self-help rural organisation founded by Canon John Hayes, a priest in the diocese of Cashel and Emly, in 1931.

While Newtown has its three successive schools intact, Portroe can lay claim to having its three police barracks in similar condition. The oldest, totally renovated, is near the bottom of the hill on the left. The second one, just beyond the church, is a neat Georgian house built originally for a daughter of William Parker of Landsdown, but later leased to the Royal Irish Constabulary and their post-1922 successors, the Garda Siochána. Finally, on the top of the hill is the purpose-built Garda Station of the mid-1970s.

Brennans pub, on the right as one ascends the hill, was the home of John/Seán Kenny (1932-73). He put Portroe on the international map in 1950 when he and three other young men crossed the Atlantic in an open ketch, the *Ituna.* The purpose of the adventure was to enable them to study under the leading American architect of the time, Frank Lloyd Wright, at his base in Arizona. After completing his studies, Kenny returned to Ireland where he worked for a some time before emigrating to London. There he directed his talents into stage design for both theatre and opera. His sets for *Oliver*, *Maggie-May*, *Pickwick*, *Hamlet*, *Uncle Vanya*, and *The Flying Dutchman* attracted as much praise and attention as the productions themselves.

The *Oliver* set won him a Tony award on Broadway in 1963. The original set is now preserved as a museum artefact in London. Sean Kenny also designed and helped to build the steel and concrete Gyrotron which was Britain's contribution to Expo 67 in Montreal.

Portroe's R.C. church was built in 1872 by Thomas Williams, Borrisoleigh, under the direction of the Parish Priest, Very Rev. Michael O'Donoghue. It is reputed to be the third church on the site. It is built of cream gritstone with sandstone corner stones in the same colour. Fr Thomas Burke, a noted Dominican, preached the opening (fundraising) sermon.

It is a single-aisle building wih gallery and timber ceiling – the latter inserted in 1914. It has two stained glass windows of high quality – probably executed by the Harry Clarke studio though neither is so inscribed. Harry Clarke (1889-1931), was an eminent Dublin-based illustrator and stained glass artist. One window depicts the Assumption of the Blessed Virgin and the other one the Sacred Heart and other aspects of Christ's life and death. The name 'W.T. Farrell' , inscribed on the bottom of one, is that of the donor of both, Rev. William T. Farrell, a native of Garrymacteige in the parish. On retirement from the Australian mission he came back to live in 'Inis Cealtra' – the bungalow he had built for himself by the cross-roads at the bottom of the village.

In the adjoining graveyard a simple headstone marks the grave of Seán Kenny and his father, Thomas J., builder and publican.

Thomas J. (Tommy) Kenny was a member of the Tipperary hurling team who made the landmark tour of the United States in 1926. In 1928 he published the diary he had kept on the tour, from the departure from Nenagh railway station of North Tipperary's eight members on 10 May 1926 for the ten-day voyage on board the *s.s. Bremen*, to their jubilant return on 27 July having played and won matches in New York, Boston, Chicago, San Francisco and Buffalo. Youghalara's Rody Nealon was one of the players and Frank McGrath the tour manager. The teams's trainer was the famous long-distance cyclist, Tim Crowe, of Dundrum, South Tipperary, who constantly wore his medals (mainly gold ones) on a belt around his waist – a sight which put some 'thieving' thoughts in some of the travellers' minds!

Edited extracts of the diary are in *Tipperary: A Treasure Chest*, a digest of historical articles, verse and anecdotes, published in 1995.

The fine national school opposite the Garda Sttion enjoys a splendid view of Lough Derg. Opened in 1971, it replaced two small schools – that at Killoran near the slate quarries which is now a Community Centre, and one in the village down the bye-road near Brennans pub.

John Nealon (1850-1912), a native of Croom, Co. Limerick, taught in the old village school. He was President of the Irish National Teachers Organisation from 1883 to 1888 and again in 1908. An illuminated address from his colleagues (now in the recreated schoolroom in Nenagh District Heritage Centre) stresses his leadership in negotiating a pension scheme for 'teachers worn out in the service'.

That included travelling to London in 1878 to meet the Chancellor of the Exchequer and the Chief Secretary for Ireland, again in 1879 to ensure the passage of the consequential Pensions Bill through the House of Commons, and publication of a pamphlet, 1904-5, seeking improvements in the scheme to the level enjoyed by teachers in England.

Charley's Hill

'Castlelough Woods, Picnic Area & Car Park, 3 km', proclaims a signpost which points down the road to the right as one reaches the highest point of the village. However, it is best to resist this sign as we will meet another road farther on which also goes to the woods.

As one rounds the next corner for the descent down Charley's Hill (so named because a Charley McCormack lived in the house at the bottom) the view ahead is dominated by Loughtea Hill (1,088 feet/331.6m) straight ahead and Tountinna (1,517 feet/462m) to the left. The object on top of Loughtea is the remains of an illuminated concrete cross erected by Very Rev. Daniel McNamara, P.P., in 1935 and which was partially destroyed by lightning some years later. Loughtea is a close variation of *lucht tighe/[land set aside for] people of a household.* Tountinna originated as *tul tuinne/the hill of the wave* [*i.e. the hill overlooking Lough Derg's waves*].

Our road, as it passes through Ballingeer and Landsdown townlands, is now sheltered by a variety of mature trees – invariably indicating the presence of a Big House. Landsdown House has an attractive, occupied lodge and a splendid wrought-iron gate and railings. The house (not visible from the road) was built by William Parker in 1779. Its weather-slated front reflects a fairly common practice in areas where there was an abundant supply of slate.

Castletown

A large advance road sign announces looming turn-offs for Castlelough Lakeside Park and the Graves of the Leinstermen. On the run-in to that Y-junction the parish's former Glebe House, or one-time residence of a Church of Ireland Rector, can be seen on the right. *Lewis's Topographical Dictionary* gives its date of building as 1820. By the roadside wall is a slate milestone, inscribed:

> Seven miles one Quarter & twenty nine perch to Nenagh. Four miles one Quarter & eleven perch to Killaloe. 1801.

The small two-storey building beside the road in front of the Glebe House is a former Protestant school of the early to mid-1880s.

A small stream under the road marks the boundary of the extensive (530 acres) townland of Castletown. The Church of Ireland parish church and graveyard lie between the two roads. Built to a design by Joseph Welland, a Board of First Fruits architect, it opened in 1855 and replaced the church in the graveyard that one sees on the way to the amenity area. This church ceased to be used for religious purposes about 1970. In 1985 it was adapted as a residence, in the process of which its original exterior appearance was altered very little. The new building near the road, which houses a garage and other rooms, is in harmony with the older design.

The fact that the church is located to one side of the site, and therefore not surrounded by gravestones, enhanced its attraction for rehabilitation as a dwelling.

A detour to Leacht an Rí Laighin, signposted to the left at the Y-junction, is optional.

Graves of the Leinstermen

To get to the 'Graves' take the left fork at the church, then go straight on for a short distance, and then take the second next road to the left. It's an uphill drive for another short distance before turning right into a narrow road (watch for the turn after the gates of Cloneybrien House on the left). The narrow road brings you to a breathtaking view of Lough Derg and to the few large slate slabs and earthen mound of a prehistoric burial site which has been telescoped in lore with the nearby burial place of a King of Leinster and his men in the late tenth or early eleventh century.

The King, accompanied by his small army, was on his way to Killaloe to seek Brian Boru's daughter in marriage. However, Gormlaith (Mrs Boru) was not in favour of such a union and, unknown to her husband, she organised an ambush on the visitors resulting in the death of all or many.

On the way to the 'Graves' one sees an exposed natural rock formation at a bend on the right of the road. One of the boulders is marked on the 1840 Ordnance Survey map as 'Knockaunreelyon' – the anglicised spelling of *cnoc an Rí Laighin/the hill/hillock of the King of Leinster.* This is the spot to which the wounded king was reputedly brought and held upright so that he could die in sight of his Leinster kingdom.

Excellent views of the redundant slate quarries are visible at different points en route.

Tountinna

Tountinna Hill, which you saw from the vantage point outside Portroe, is easily accessible by continuing on past the 'graves' and taking the first road on your left (the turn-off can be difficult enough to negotiate) off which a short distance on is a road to the summit. But to really savour the view one should leave the car or bicycle near the bottom of that road and walk up. Local people still cut and harvest turf on top of the hill and there is fish a-plenty in the Black Lough. If you are driving it is advisable to return to the main road at the church-cum-residence rather than be tempted to follow any Ballina signpost as the road is extremely narrow for two-way traffic.

An alternative to the drive to the top is to ascend via the Lough Derg Way path near the Fógra Poiblí (public notice) and enjoy the splendid scenery as it opens up gradually; the hillside has at least four varieties of heather, several species of ferns and other peat-loving plants.

However, the virtual equivalent of the above spectacular view is available on the main road at the Lookout, a little over a quarter of a mile on from the signpost at the Y-junction on the main road.

Before the Lookout there is another recommended detour: the graveyard and Lakeside Park (pictured on page 43) and woods, all down to the right.

Graveyard, Lakeside Park, and Woods

The Park has parking, picnic and toilet facilities, and a children's play area with slides, swings and sand. There's also a short lakeside walk. Portroe Muintir na Tíre were responsible for acquisition of the site from the Land Commission, and Tipperary (N.R.) Co. Council for its development.

Castletown graveyard contains the finest collection of decorated gravestones in north-west Tipperary. Slate's durability, and its suitability for carving, is clearly demonstrated here. A local group recently did a thorough clean-up of the grounds, uncovering many buried stones and in the process creating a virtual folk-art gallery (see rear flap).

The area's links with the slate quarrying area of North Wales can be gleaned from a perusal of some of the gravestone inscriptions – Sir Henry Warren Brooke (d. 1859) and Maurice Morris (d. 1839) from Beaumaris and Bangor respectively. Close to the rear external wall of the church is the raised flat stone of Griffith Parry, Quarryman, also from Bangor, who died at Curraghbally in 1847. The Welsh inscription on the stone was translated as follows by a visitor to Nenagh District Heritage Centre:

> Truly famous man of Gwynedd – Peace
> (in) Jesus
> Lies here below,
> Strong in friendship was he,
> Pure splendour be the respect of his
> grave.
> Dewi Union

The Parkers

The name Parker is synonymous with Castletown and Castlelough. A John Parker of Dunkipp, Co. Limerick, and his wife Alice, are mentioned in a 1709 document relating to the manor of Castletownarra. The oldest fully-legible inscribed gravestone to this family in Castletown is dated 1800 and commemorates an Anthony born in 1737 – he is probably the man who hosted Arthur Young, the touring English agriculturist, in 1777 and whose reclamation of some 40 acres of land so impressed Young.

There is another Anthony of Castletown also buried here, whose lifespan was 1769-1837.

Anthony J. (1845-1905), son of Rev. Standish Grady Parker and Margaret Gabbett, was a notable public figure, being a member of Tipperary's North Riding's grand jury up to its replacement by the first elected County Council in 1899.

He made local history by being one of only two landlords elected to that first council and the only one returned unopposed. The nationalist candidate selected for the Derrycastle electoral division withdrew after a vigorous spate of pro-and anti-Parker letters in the local newspapers. Anthony J. married Anna Christina Hutchinson, Timoney, Roscrea. She died in 1871, aged only 24 years. Their son, Standish Grady John Parker (1870-1937) received royal permission in 1891 to take the arms of Hutchinson and thereafter the family name was Parker Hutchinson.

The ruin in the graveyard is that of the parish's old Protestant church. There is an ancient flat tomb, with raised lettering, right up against the outside of its north wall which may well have been inside the walls of the parish's earlier pre-Reformation church prior to its reconstruction sometime in the 1700s for use by the local Church of Ireland community. The stone marks the burial place of Morine Carrol, wife of Terence Mac I Brien. Their son,

Muircheartach, was Protestant Bishop of Killaloe, 1575-1613.

Past the graveyard are the remains of a tower house with later additions. The *Civil Survey* of 1654 has a good description of the complement of buildings in the vicinity of the parish church:

> … the Castle of Castletowne situated close by the Shannon, together with a barbican & a Slate house has alsoe a Garden and an Orchard a water mill and eight thatch tennements …[A barbican is a projecting wall tower].

This updated tower house would appear to qualify as the 'manor house at Castletown' which 'commanded a view of the 'mighty Shennan … ' occupied by Maurice/Mortimus Mac I Brien, the future Bishop of Killaloe, in 1573 (according to Canon Philip Dwyer's *The Diocese of Killaloe* (1878)).

The 1840 Ordnance Survey Sheet for Co. Tipperary No. 19 shows an old mill opposite the graveyard and its gable and side walls still survive in the trees; it appears to have been only one-storey high. Only archaeological investigation will determine if it is of seventeenth-century vintage. The stream which powered it is still gushing along and one of its large grinding stones is preserved as a feature in a nearby garden.

Woodlands Walk

Castlelough Woods lies about a half mile beyond the amenity area. On the way one passes Castlelough House. Part of the house dates from the early eighteenth century and fits the description of the one in which Arthur Young stayed in 1777 which he described as ' … so near the river as to be sometimes washed by it'. The builder was most likely the John Parker referred to above, or his descendant. An impressive south-facing wing was added by the Parker owner in the next century.

The woodland walk, developed under the auspices of the commercial arm of the Department of Energy, Coillte Teoranta, was opened in June 1989 by Michael Smith, T.D., Minister for Energy. It is a most welcome amenity containing optional 2km and 3km circular walks. Its accessibility, length, and proximity to the lake, enhance the attractions of this area enormously. The only requirement for the walker is a pair of strong shoes. Refreshments to baptise the picnic seats and binoculars to study the wild life and scenery will add to the enjoyment.

Again, Peggy and Siobhán Geraghty have produced an illustrated leaflet for this walk. It draws attention to the old stone wall which enclosed the long-gone deer park of Castlelough House, to oak trees surviving from the deer park, and to other species like hazel, holly, alder, beech, birch and conifer.

Primroses, wood anemones, violets and wood sorrel are there in profusion, while crab apples and the berries of the holly and ivy support a large population of birds. The lake has mute swans, crested grebes, moorhens and cormorants at this point.

In the shallow bays one sees yellow water lilies, bog beans, reedmace, bull rushes, common reeds and marsh marigolds. The verges of the broad paths have plenty of foxgloves, ferns, St. John's Wort, and a variety of mosses and lichen.

Back to the main road now for the drive past the spectacular viewing point called the Lookout (see photograph on page 43). You are bound to be one of the tens of thousands who pause there annually.

Ionad Radhairce/Lookout

The road you are now following is not marked on the 1840 Ordnance Survey Sheet. The road to Ballina was then the up-hill left fork of the Y-junction. A new short stretch of road, nearer the lake, was built in 1860-2. It joins up with the old road a short distance beyond the viewing point. The contractor was a James Gleeson and he was paid 19*s* 6*d* (97.5p) per perch, the equivalent of £312 per mile.

The view at the Lookout encompasses Co. Clare's Slieve Bernagh range of hills and a considerable extent of that county's lakeside shoreline. Scarriff Bay, with the distinctive Inis Cealtra/Holy Island, is almost opposite you. The round tower is one of several ecclesiastical ruins. Saints Caimin and also Colum of Terryglass are associated with the island. For a brief history of Inis Cealtra read the *Guide to Mountshannon* by Thomas V. MacNamara, P.P., but for more detail get Gerard Madden's *Holy Island.*

There is evidence of continuous religious activity on the island from the Early Christian period right down to the present – it is still used as a parish burial ground. Mountshannon is the third village one meets after Killaloe on the Co. Clare lake drive. It won the national Tidy Towns overall award some years ago. Boat trips to Holy Island are available from Mountshannon's fine harbour. Trips are also organised by the East Clare Heritage Centre in Tuamgraney. The latter area was the birthplace of well-known author Edna O'Brien and it has figured in some of her novels and short stories.

You get a splendid aerial view of Castletown graveyard, the Lakeside Park and its hinterland, with the Scilly islands in the water immediately below you. Most of the land was part of Parker's Castlelough House demesne until acquired and divided by the Land Commission in the late 1950s.

The slope below us may well be the reclaimed land described by Arthur Young. 'It was once covered with ling and furze ... He [Parker] grubbed and ploughed it and sowed oats and marled the stubble from the Shannon. ... Upon this he took a crop of wheat and another of oats and with the latter sowed the seeds of grass.'

There is a short forest walk beside the viewing point, or one can cross the road to another forest path and climb to enjoy the panoramic scenery from a higher level.

Two features of the remainder of the journey will be the constant view of the lake to the right and the exclusive use of slate stone as a building material for older dwellings, out-buildings, walls and entrances. The route generally is a rich one for persons with an interest in vernacular architecture and industrial archaeology – quarries, mills, quays.

The pink wash of Loughtea House makes it a distinctive landmark for lake traffic. This neat Georgian house (on the right) was a slate quarry manager's residence. The entrance is, as one would expect, constructed of slate. There is a quay down below where bundles of slate, quarried in the hills to our left, were loaded onto boats for transport to distant customers.

At the next viewing point you see the lakeside trees of Derrycastle estate below and the tip of Tinarana House across the lake. The solid two-storey farmhouse on the left is also worth noting. It was built by James Joy in the early 1820s. James was a stonemason by profession and came to this area from Co. Waterford. In 1828 he leased 26 acres in Townlough Upper (pronounced Tomlough in speech) from Helen Maria Rolleston. His descendants still occupy the house and land.

The sale of Rolleston land in the Encumbered Estates Courts in 1854 brought an end to that family's connection with the area since their ancestor, Francis, received a grant of land hereabouts in the Cromwellian period. A descendant, Charles Rolleston, Q(ueen's) C(ounsel) (born 1807), Glasshouse, Shinrone, Co. Offaly, was a notable nineteenth-century defence counsel (he defended the Cormack Brothers). T(homas) W(illiam) Rolleston (1857-1920), the noted scholar, journalist and author, was his son.

Derrycastle

Clancy's Bridge, with its left metal parapet visible and its right stone one totally occluded by brambles, spans a fast-flowing stream from the foothills of Tountinna. Clancy's house alongside lies vacant. Once over the bridge one is in Templeachally/Ballina parish and cruising between the townlands of Derrybeg (left) and Derry Demesne (right). Derry is the anglicised form of *doire/oak wood.*

An ivy-clad wall of slate slabs on the right leads one to a newly-created entrance to the former Derrycastle House of which only some out-buildings and a walled garden survive. The main, magnificent entrance is farther on.

Samuel Wade of the Cromwellian/Parliamentary forces, received substantial grants of O'Brien lands hereabouts in lieu of arrears of pay. He was one of the 'most humble and obliged servants' who signed an address presented to Ireland's Lord Lieutenant, James Butler, the first Duke of Ormonde, in March 1670. Wade and the other signatories had obviously taken up residence on their grants and were anxious to have them made secure by Royal approval since the regime they had supported was now ended and Charles II had been restored to the English throne.

Elizabeth Wade, Samuel's descendant, married John Head of Waterford and began the Head dynasty at Derrycastle. Michael Head, who hosted Arthur Young in 1777, was married to Margaret Prittie, sister to the first Baron Dunalley of Kilboy.

Michael and Margaret's son, Michael Prittie Head (1770-1836), is buried in Castletown Church of Ireland graveyard. His daughter, Henrietta, displayed considerable mettle in June 1837. She brought a case against 28-year-old Simon George Purdon of Tinarana House across the lake in Co. Clare for a breach of promise of marriage. They had been engaged for eleven years but in August 1836, about a month after her father's death, Simon G. upped and married Louisa Ponsonby, a daughter of the Bishop of Derry. The jury awarded Henrietta £3,000 damages, worth approximately £195,000 of today's pounds. The *Clare Journal*, at her request, did not publish a report of the case.

Henrietta's generation of Heads got into financial difficulties and in August 1840 the estate (4,500 acres), then owned by her brother Michael Henry Head, was put up for sale by public auction. Two bold assertions in the auction prospectus were: (a) [that] 'the use of spirituous liquors was unknown throughout the vast district' and (b) 'an immediate additional income is within reach by those who have money at their command by building 50 or 100 villas on the banks of the lake ...' The extensive slate quarries, plus copper and lead deposits, on the estate, were also highlighted as was its proximity to the river Shannon, described as 'far famed and one of the finest rivers in the Empire'.

70,000 guineas (£73,500 or £16.33p per acre – approximately £1,000 per acre in1990s' pounds) were bid at the auction by an unnamed bidder but the *Nenagh Guardian* thought that 'Mr Guinness was interested'. Francis Spaight of Limerick was the eventual purchaser. Spaights were timber, corn and coal importers and the owners of a fleet of steamers which conveyed cargo and passengers around the world.

His son, William Spaight (1807-1889), inherited. But tragedy betook him with the death of his only two children in adulthood and the accidental destruction of the house by fire in 1872 in which two youths, Michael O'Meara (18) and John Dwyer (16), lost their lives. The house was not restored but William continued to live in a smaller dwelling on the estate until his sudden death in 1889. Like most large estates it was eventually acquired and divided by the Land Commission. In time the ruined house was demolished but its portico was salvaged and now fronts Parteen House near Limerick.

The garden wall, constructed of slate slabs, is as straight as a die and is one of the finest examples of the craft of the stone mason to be seen in this area.

From this secondary entrance an extensive wall of slate slabs, now almost hidden by ivy and brambles, leads to the main entrance of Derrycastle House. Here one sees a refurbished and enlarged lodge and a noble pair of gates and railings (all privately owned). The avenue was about 1.75 miles (2.8 km) long and serviced the house and a fruit grove, a quay, cottages on the estate, and then continued on to another entrance beside Clancy's Bridge which facilitated journeys to Portroe and beyond.

Derry Castle/tower house, from which the Big House took its name, stood on land owned by Teige O'Brien of Tuogh (now Cappamore and in Tipperary South) per the *Civil Survey* of 1654. The surveyors described it thus: ' ... a little castle with a little Bawne about it on an island in ye Shannon, it wants repayre'. That description from almost 350 years ago still applies – for there it stands peeping through the ivy at fishermen and other lake travellers.

'Michael Range'

The road continues to be lined with trees and walls until interrupted by another remarkable entrance in Ryninch townland. This leads to Michael Range Wildlife Sanctuary and Aviation Village. Twentieth-century stonemasons have created a wide sweep made of slate slabs and utilised a huge boulder of slate as a piece of modern sculpture.

Local people can recall the controversy which the proposed plans for Michael Range generated in the early 1980s with opposition coming from environmental, angling and other groups. The plan proposed the development of a 'self-sufficient complex' on a 92-acre lakeside site. It would have organic farms, home-produced energy and a Centre with meeting, training, recreational and residential facilities. This Centre was to be built into a natural amphitheatre right beside the water with underground fuel tanks and quays nearby.

None of the proposed development went ahead other than the building of a harbour. The land is now a wildlife sanctuary. Red deer are bred and raised in free-range conditions here.

The location of Michael Range's near neighbour, Katie Daly's, also came in for a fair share of criticism. Built in the 1970s, when isolated, licensed halls were still in fashion, and named for the 'mountain dew' distiller, heroine of a popular American country and western song, its prominent siting and 'loud' architecture found favour with few.

The road moves away from the lake now and past houses with an urban flavour – but there are at least two old-style ones with extensions in harmony with the original; one is approached via a grand sweep of slate slabs and has a magnificent heather garden.

Ballina-Killaloe: Heritage Town

Ballina

A speed limit sign signals the approach of Ballina (*béal an átha/the mouth of the ford; called in ancient annals 'átha na borumha'*: the *ford of/where the tribute or tax of cows [was paid]*. On the right is the entrance to a mooted holiday home development of the early 1980s which did not come to fruition. The builders of the entrance were not, unfortunately, as environmentally-conscious as those who did the Michael Range one.

Over on the left are two very new but separate schemes of detached houses. Ashgrove Meadows has a complement of thirty detached houses and Ivy Grove has fifteen. Retailing between £63,000 and £67,000, they were quickly taken up for permanent family homes.

After negotiating the bend by the entrance to Ballina GAA Club grounds and pavilion, the approach to the village is marked with a fountain painted in the county colours of blue and gold, private and local authority houses and, straight ahead, a view of the tower of Killaloe Cathedral. Behind the hedges Lough Derg's expansive area of water has narrowed to become the River Shannon again.

Templeachally is the original name of this parish (the R.C parish is called Ballina-Boher and comprises all of Templeachally and part of Kilmastulla parishes). The name Chapel Lane still survives in local use for the entrance to one of the private dwellings on the right – thus pinpointing for posterity the location of an early parish church. A fine cream sandstone house, behind a high wall, catches the eye.

Ballina town has a population of 477. Again, you will see a signpost for the Lough Derg Way.

A rail link from the Waterford-Limerick line to Killaloe, via Birdhill, came into operation in April 1862. The railway, like the slate quarries, favoured the well-known name of Killaloe and put it on their timetables though the line did not actually cross the river but had its terminus on the Tipperary side.

At first the line terminated downriver from the bridge and the station was there. Then it was extended to new station buildings, now refurbished as a restaurant and a private house, which can be seen on the way to the Lakeside Hotel. Finally, it was extended a good distance beyond that to a goods store.

The Lakeside Hotel first opened in 1900 but was rebuilt in the mid-1920s after being destroyed by fire. It has undergone major refurbishment and extension in recent years to include a leisure centre with an indoor swimming pool, play area and creche. Development behind the hotel is ongoing; there are holiday homes, a fine marina with extensive berthage, a terminal point for cruiser-hire and a floatel.

A waterbus provides hour-long trips on the river and lake on a regular basis during the Summer and takes off from the new jetty between the bridge and the former station buildings.

The stretch of river above the bridge is ideal for water-sking, a sport which was introduced here in the late 1950s.

Downstream of the bridge the course of the redundant railway line has been developed as a riverside walk, car park and swimming pool. A lounge bar was for some years named 'North Riding' – the only such use of the administrative county's name. Some of the red sandstone slabs which decorate the front have interesting markings on them.

The area provided inspiration for Sergeant Jack Keily's prolific pen during the few years he served here prior to his promotion to Head Constable and transfer to Mountrath R.I.C. station in 1897.

Verse tributes to the new railway station, the parish's curate, a girl called Mary who acquired one of the first Dunlop-shod bicycles, and the village fountain appeared in Nenagh's newspapers. He also penned a poignant tribute to six-year-old Pete Malone who was tragically swept away as he tried his hand at fishing in 1895.

Many a torch illumes the wave
But no trace of Pete is found
His name brings back no answer save
The murmuring river's sound.
His parents call and their hearts beat wild,
Yet not a word from their missing child.

Ballina-Killaloe enjoys the designation of Heritage Town. This is more than an honour – the twin towns are included in a specialised Bord Fáilte/ Irish Tourist Board's marketing programme, are eligible for European Union funds earmarked for heritage projects. However, the initiative for development must come from the community.

The results of their efforts are already in evidence – additional jetties and angling facilities, tasteful restoration of old buildings, and erection of interpretative panels with text and illustrations recounting aspects of the towns' history. There is a printed heritage trail in three languages and an annual festival is held in July.

In the vicinity of the R.C. parish church in Ballina one can savour the lovely view downriver and across the thirteen-arched bridge which links the two towns. This is a favourite target of photographers (see page 44). The church is built of cream sandstone; it has no datestone but is thought to have been built in the early 1840s. Inside there are representations in stained glass of Saints Brigid, Ailbe, Peter, and Teresa of Lisieux. McKeogh is the most common name on the gravestones in the adjoining graveyard.

Hydro-Electric Scheme

Up to 1929 when the Shannon Hydro-Electric Scheme was initiated by the government of the day, the river at Ballina-Killaloe presented a different appearance to that seen now. Old geography books describe Killaloe as a 'waterfall town', for here the river cascaded over huge boulders and fell 98ft (30m) between here and Limerick. A canal was cut in 1799 to bypass the rapids. Deepening of the river bed, removal of the rocks and other obstacles, and insertion of weirs and sluices were undertaken in the 1840s, 1880s and 1890s. Finally, in 1925-9 the bed was deepened again, and the water level raised, during the harnessing of the river for Ireland's first major Hydro-Electric Scheme. This development saw the old canal submerged and low-lying land below Killaloe flooded to create a large lake.

A weir and intake was constructed on the river at Parteen Villa 3 miles (4.8km) south of Killaloe Bridge to divert the water and control the flow into a 7.5 mile (12km) canal or headrace which carries the large volume of water downstream to Ardnacrusha in Co. Clare. Here a 100 foot (30m) high dam feeds 4 pinstocks or pipes which convey the water to the turbines in the power station.

The Parteen weir has sluice gates to control the flow of water into the headrace and the old river bed, plus a navigation gate and fish pass.

Having generated the electricity the water then enters a 1.5 mile (2.4km) canal, or tailrace, and is carried off to rejoin the parent river.

Another navigation pass at the power station facilitates river traffic ranging from canoes to cruisers going to and from Limerick (the hire cruisers do not go beyond Killaloe). There is a Visitor Centre at this most environmentally-friendly power station with pictorial displays, a video and guided tour. Admission is free.

As Lough Derg is actually a reservoir for the hydro-electric scheme its water level can be raised and lowered by the E(lectricty) S(upply) B(oard).

Back on *terra firma* and a short distance beyond Ballina R.C. church, there is an older graveyard in the grounds of the parish's pre-Reformation church; here one can see some twelfth-century features inserted in a later (circa fifteenth-century) building.

Templeachally (*teampall an cala/the church of the callow or low, marshy meadow near the river*), is the burial place of the O'Hickeys, physicians to the O'Briens, MacNamaras and O'Kennedys, but their tomb is no longer identifiable. Young Pete Malone was buried here over a century ago.

Killaloe

Having toured Ballina you now cross the bridge to Killaloe. Half-way across you will see a tablet commemorating four victims of the War of Independence – Michael MacEgan, Martin MacMahon, Martin Gildea and Alphonsus

Rodgers, summarily shot here by Crown forces on 16 November 1920 following their arrest up-lake at Williamstown.

The Tourist Information Office, which has an exhibition area, is conveniently located on the right at the end of the bridge on the Killaloe side.

Killaloe has a population of 956. It has a primary school and post-primary Community College. The town's location in a 'cut-away' hill gives character and some air of mystery to its streets and lanes. It is a town for cyclists and walkers rather than drivers. A one-way street system is in operation.

Main Street has some fine examples of traditional shop fronts. Those of John Crotty merit study, particularly for their porcelain lettering, the fruit carved on the consoles or brackets, and how cleverly those shop fronts are designed to cope with the steep slope of the street. The town also has some very attractive houses, some with unrendered sandstone facades.

Immediately downstream of the bridge is an eel weir – a series of metal posts from which nets are hung during the eel-fishing season from October to February. The eels are then stored in floating cages sited in the eel house (on the right bank) which is located half on land and half in the water.

Pike angling is highly developed here; there are several well-organised challenge competitions. First-class facilities are available by way of sheltered cat walks and boats, hotel, guesthouse and self-catering accommodation.

Killaloe's history has been well documented by local historian Sean Kierse, and his publications *Historic Killaloe – a guide to its antiquities,* and *Portraits of Killaloe* (fifty photographs with captions) are a must for the serious explorer and for the hurried visitor who will appreciate a later armchair refresher.

The placename is specific to a person, as are a minority of placenames, in this case *cill da Lua/the church of Lua.* St. Lua built his monastery on an island in the river.

Killaloe was chosen as the ecclesiastical centre when dioceses were defined in the twelfth century. St. Flannan's Oratory and Cathedral take the viewer back in time to that period. St. Flannan (died 778) was a native of the area.

The cathedral dates from the thiteenth century and stands on the site of an earlier Romanesque building destroyed by fire in 1185. After the Reformation it passed into Protestant ownership and became the seat of the first Protestant bishop of the diocese, Muircheartach O Brien, whose name was already mentioned in connection with Castletown graveyard.

One of the chief architectural features of the cathedral is the magnificent Hiberno-Romanesque doorway rescued from the destroyed church and inserted in the south wall of its successor.

A unique stone is preserved here – the only known example of a stone inscribed with both Irish Ogham and Scandinavian Runes. The Runic has been translated as 'Thorgrim carved this cross' and the Ogham as 'a blessing upon Thorgrim'. It has been dated to circa AD 1000.

DROMINEER: from the 14th century to the 21st – a hub of activity.

GARRYKENNEDY: recreation and recuperation.

LOOKOUT: on (nearer to viewer, l to r) Aughinish Point, the Scilly Islands; (closer to Clare shore, l to r) Holy Island, Bushy Island; the Slieve Bernagh hills.

CASTLETOWN graveyard and lakeside park.

BALLINA-KILLALOE: cathedral, busy bridge and eel weir, railway line turned riverside walk, sun-shot and cloud-swept hills.

O'KENNEDY COUNTRY: Puckane's holiday cottages combine modern comfort with traditional craft; Lisquillibeen tower house recalls medieval glory.

Bustling Borrisokane and Lorrha's monastic memorials span more than a millenium of changing lifestyles.

TERRYGLASS: a quiet street where new friends meet; in front of the craft shop and gallery – lupins and delphiniums, roses and lavender, poppies and pansies and lilies in the Old Church entrance garden.

PORTUMNA: cruisers surge from the swivel bridge; a group is guided through the newly-restored de Burgo Castle.

The cathedral itself has a wealth of features – corbels, capitals, stained glass, timber work, and brass and marble wall memorials. The one beside the pulpit commemorates Civil Engineer, John Grantham (1775-1833), first surveyor of the River Shannon and the man who put the first steamboat on it in 1825. The cathedral is the location for occasional music and choral recitals. An informative leaflet is available in its shop and guided tours can be arranged.

The oratory, which is a well-preserved nave of a twelfth-century Romanesque church, has a decorated west doorway (right) and a vaulted ceiling, above which is an overcroft under a high-pitched roof of stones (not slate).

King Brian Boru

It is an uphill walk from all directions to the Roman Catholic church which sits atop the town's highest point. Ceann Coradh/ Kincora, the birthplace and royal palace of Brian Boru covered this area but no trace of it is now discernible.

Brian warred successfully against the Limerick Vikings, and against native opposition to gain the High Kingship of Ireland in 1002. He led an Irish-Viking alliance against the King of Leinster and his Dublin Viking allies in the battle of Clontarf in 1014. But he was not destined to enjoy his triumph for he was killed by a fleeing Viking while resting in his tent after the battle.

An ongoing struggle for power between Brian's son and successor, Donchad, and Donchad's nephew, Toirdealbhach, divided and weakened the O'Brien dynasty, making Kincora an easy target for other enemies. But it survived to witness the defeat of uncle by nephew and accession of the nephew's son to the High Kingship. His death in 1119, after a turbulent and warring lifetime, spurred the vengeful O'Brien enemy, Turlough O'Connor from the western province of Connaught, to attack and finally destroy the historic palace.

St. Flannan and St. Lua

At the R.C. church the visitor will see that it too has a small oratory in its grounds. St. Lua's Oratory consists of nave and chancel and is of ninth or tenth-century vintage. It was dismantled and removed here from its natural home on Friar's Island, a small island in the Tipperary side of the river downstream from the bridge, before the island vanished under the rising waters of the hydro-electric scheme.

Like St. Flannan's oratory, it has a stone roof – on the chancel only – with a very small chamber underneath. The building's features are plain and undecorated.

The R.C. church is also dedicated to St. Flannan, which explains why there are two 'St. Flannan' fingerposts pointing in opposite directions – one towards it and one towards the cathedral/oratory. Tablets within the R.C. church commemorate two diocesan bishops who chose Killaloe as their place of residence – Right Rev. Nicholas Power (died 1871) and Right Rev. James Ryan (1806-1889). The stained glass window on the left of the altar is from the Harry Clarke studio and depicts St. Patrick in bishop's robes. The three-panelled window on the right, though unsigned, appears to be from the same studio. It depicts the Annunciation, the Presentation in the Temple, and the Flight into Egypt.

And when I put about and steer, back for the walls of Dromineer,
Then, far on the horizon's line, the pillar tower of Caimin's shrine
From out the water rears on high its finger in the western sky;
'Tis thirteen hundred years agone, since thence the sacred lightnings shone
Throughout three nights on Shannon's foam to light the corse of Colum home,
From Inis Cealtra o'er the wave to Tír dhá Ghlas, his chosen grave.

– from 'The Place Where I Was Born', by Dermot F. Gleeson

To Portumna

The traveller from Nenagh to Portumna has a choice of routes for part of the way – via the main road through Ardcroney and Borrisokane to Carrigahorig, or along the eastern shore of Lough Derg via Puckane, Coolbawn, Ballinderry and Terryglass which is the route chosen for this guide.

There is also a choice of two exit routes from the town when one commences the journey from Banba Square in front of the Courthouse.

Via St. Joseph's Park

Firstly, the shorter of those two exit routes: this goes past the Gatehouse of the former County Gaol, now part of Nenagh District Heritage Centre. This is at the entrance to the town's Convent of Mercy.

The local Community of the Sisters of Mercy leased the redundant gaol complex in 1887 for educational purposes and later built their convent and schools within its confines.

The octagonal building seen through the archway has a varied history. It housed successive gaol Governors and their families from its completion in 1842 until adapted for convent purposes. After the Sisters moved to their purpose-built convent in 1913 it became a girls' post-primary school and functioned as such until 1981. Since then it has been adapted as a local history museum under the direction of a voluntary body, Nenagh District Heritage Society.

The impressive Gatehouse of the gaol is at the archway. It too is part of the Heritage Centre and is open to visitors. During the lifetime of the gaol it had three functions – as the reception area for prisoners and visitors coming and going; accommodation for up to four prisoners under sentence of death; and the site of execution by hanging.

When the Sisters of Mercy took over the complex they installed their caretaker here. Today, as well as being part of the Heritage Centre, its ground floor houses Tipperary North Family History Foundation's research centre. This centre is part of the countrywide (32-county) network of centres set up in recent years under Irish Genealogy Ltd. Here and elsewhere a database has been created of all the principal genealogical records (births/baptisms, marriages, deaths, burials, land records, gravestone inscriptions and the 1901 census) for each centre's catchment area – which in this case is Tipperary North Riding. There is a similar one in Cashel for the South Riding. The centre here has over three-quarters of a million records in its database and gives a fast efficient service. However, it is not a 'do it yourself' centre – research is done for you on a fee basis.

Also worthy of note on this route are the beautiful gates and church of St. Mary's of the Rosary; the thirteenth-century Norman (Butler) castle; the girls National School (1911) which supports a school band and majorettes; the boys National School (1914); St. Conlan's Welfare Home (1975); and a new branch library (1996). Information on all of these is found in this guide's companion volume, *Walkabout Nenagh.*

This road was once called Gaol Street but now bears the more dignified one of O'Rahilly – after Kerry native, The (Michael Joseph) O'Rahilly (1875-1916) of the Irish Volunteers, killed in action during the 1916 Rising in Dublin. It merges with St. Flannan's Street at the water pump. Looking to the right from there you can see the Church of Ireland national/primary school of 1906, considerably extended in 1976. It has two teachers and 39 pupils.

The next right turn takes one into the New Line of 1860 and past St. Joseph's Park. This estate of 1936 vintage has 111 houses and was the Urban District Council's first large-scale scheme specifically earmarked to re-house residents living in the town's principal lanes. In 1974 the residents took the initiative in the provision and furnishing of a children's playground (to your left) on a site purchased by themselves. The attractive mural in the playground was painted some years ago by pupils of St. Mary's Secondary School.

The New Line was bereft of commercial development until the advent of the 'cash & carry' on the left and the funeral home on the right. The concept of using a funeral home, instead of the deceased's own home with a traditional wake, found favour very slowly in rural towns but is now common practice.The rumble strips were inserted in the road surface in an effort to curb the speed of the ever-increasing volume of traffic through this highly-populated area

The New Line meets up with the Borrisokane Road – the route used by Galway-Limerick traffic; *your read resumes at 'Development', p.54.*

[Alternative Route]: Via the Streets

Traffic lights dictate the pace of progress on the second route from Banba Square. We go first through Kickham Street, formerly Peter Street.

As the only access from the town's main street, to the field wherein the new courthouse and gaol were to be sited, was the narrow Bachelor's Walk, this new and wider street was cut parallel to it in 1839. It was called Peter Street after the town's landlord Peter Holmes,Jun. His name was replaced by that of Fenian and writer, Charles J. Kickham of Mullinahone in the South Riding, in 1920. Kickham's name was retained in the referendum of 1965.

1996 saw the restoration of a landmark. Nenagh Credit Union Offices began life in the last century as a typical Corn and Wool stores. Successive owners were John F. Tumpane, Frank R. Maloney and Frank McGrath. We encountered the two Franks on the Ballina-Killaloe route. Prior to its restoration the building was a fuel retail outlet. A branch of the Credit Union was opened in Nenagh in 1971.

The Garda Station, renovated and expanded by the Office of Public Works was a branch of the Provincial Bank which came to Nenagh in 1856.

A left turn now takes you into Pearse Street, or Castle Street as it was called until 1920.

Two eye-catching buildings on the left, Dun Mhuire and the Lecture Hall, date from 1883 and 1869, respectively. Go straight through at the traffic lights and into Summerhill.

Walkabout Nenagh has a wealth of information on the houses and personalities of Summerhill: the *Nenagh Guardian* newspaper (No. 13) and the associated and brilliant O'Shea family; the Georgian terrace including No. 21, once home of a distinguished Gleeson family, one of whom, Dermot, has left a fine body of local history writing, notably *The Last Lords of Ormond* (1938; Relay, 1997) which relates the story of the Cromwellian land confiscations in the territory through which you are heading; the Christian Brothers' schools and the neighbouring Summerville House (1836) and its former residents; likewise, the former home of both John Hanly, the courthouse, gaol and military barracks (left) builder, and Dr Ned Sheehan, writer of *Nenagh and its Neighbourhood*. The former barracks (1832) and neighbouring houses and a new street to the right are similarly treated in *Walkabout Nenagh*. The barracks, a noteworthy building recessed from the

street, stands on a triangular fortified site. It had accommodation for a company of 246 men.

The former name of Ormond Street, which begins beyond the barracks, was Old Turnpike Road, implying that a toll-gate was in operation at one time – the gate was located at the next junction where the road to the right goes to Birr via Modreeney, the Pike and Loughkeen.

This road, like most of the town's other streets, answers to two names – Birr and Bulfin. The inspiration for the first is obvious. William Bulfin (1864-1910) was born near Birr, emigrated to Argentina and owned a newspaper in Buenos Aires. On his return to Ireland in 1902 he commenced a bicycle tour of the country and he subsequently recorded his impressions and experiences in *Rambles in Erin* (1907).

The house on the upper corner is the former Crescent Nursing Home where Brendan Graham, of Eurovision Song contest fame, was born. The home, which catered for maternity and acute medical cases, was run by his mother's cousins, Bridget (Dilly) and Mary Ann (Bab) Starr. Brendan Graham's achievement has been extraordinary in four times composing the Irish entry for the Eurovision song contest over a twenty-year span. His composition won the contest in 1994 and again in 1996 to bring Ireland's total wins to six.

On the opposite side of the road entrance a stone nameplate on the corner house reads, 'Harkness Place 1877'. The builder of the terrace of nine houses which extends down the hill and around the corner into Birr Road, was James D. Harkness who had a hardware business in the town's main street.

Down the hill, Sallygrove, the housing estate on the right, has been appropriately named, for Paddy O'Connor grew sallies/willows here for his Nenagh basket-making industry in the 1940s and '50s. The Nenagh river is but a field away behind the houses and a goodly crop of willow trees have seeded themselves along the banks. The meeting point of the Nenagh and Ollatrim rivers is also along there.

Development

The buildings at the junction of the New Line and the Borrisokane road housed Nenagh Textiles (carpets, towelling and tapestry furnishing fabrics). This industry, established in 1953 by the Vandenberghe family, Belgium, was an important cog in the town's industrial wheel until its closure in December 1989. Happily, the buildings found a new life as Banaghan's warehouse and showrooms – toys, stationery, fancy goods and cards. Part of it served as a temporary fire station until the erection of the purpose-built one on the Limerick road.

The office block and houses alongside are further evidence of urban expansion. This was a green field and home to North Tipperary Show Committee's annual show on 15 August until 1983. Between the shows sheep grazed the fields, which also served as a training ground for athletes – as did the horticultural hall during the winter months.

The once-green fields on the other side have undergone great change too. Following the sally growing an innovative amenity – an eighteen hole pitch-and-putt course – flourished there for a few years until the club which sprang up as a result spread its wings and developed its own course. Sally beds and putting greens are long submerged 'neath houses, gardens and supermarket.

Brookwatson

At the verge of the town beech trees mark the entrance (on the right) to Brookwatson, the youthful home of John Desmond Bernal (1901-1971), Scientific Adviser to the Chief of Combined Operations (U.K.) during World War II, awarded the Lenin Peace Prize in 1953, and author of seven books. His younger brother, Kevin O'C(arroll) (1903-1996) stayed home and made his mark as an extensive dairy farmer, Independent Urban District Councillor (1950-74), and long-time photographer. The interest in photography was inherited from his father, Samuel Bernal, whose pictures of Nenagh street scenes, St. Mary's of the Rosary church under construction (1892-6), and family portraits appear in *Nenagh Yesterday* (1993). So do some of Kevin's more recent ones; he was photographer for the *Nenagh Guardian* during the 1950s, '60s and '70s.

Carty's Cross is a notable landmark. A development at this point is the Travellers' Halting Site, with room for five to six families, provided by Tipperary (N.R.) Co. Council. Further on is the Showgrounds developed by the Show Committee to replace the one on the verge of the town. 1996 saw part of the new acquisition sold to an agricultural contractor. However, the annual show, changed from its traditional date of 15 August to a Sunday in July, is still held here.

St. John's Well is signposted down a pathway beside the Nenagh river, to the right just short of the bridge. Here, in the name of St. John, the rites of Mid-Summer's Eve (24 June) became subsumed into a Christian pilgrimage on that day which continues as an annual parish Mass.

Worthy of note alongside the well is a massive oak tree. Its circumference at the base is approximately 18 feet (5.5m) and 13 feet (4m) at shoulder height. Its branches span out to about 80 feet (over 24m).

As of the 1970s a new bridge spans the Nenagh river which is wending its way to the river Shannon at Dromineer. It is still called Scott's Bridge after the Samuel Scott, followed by his son Willie, who worked the corn mill in the last and this century. The redundant bridge is still intact. This was also the site of the manor mill of Nenagh. One finds references to it in medieval deeds and in later leases where the agreements contain 'covenants to do suit and service at the Court Leet and grind Corn at the Mill of Nenagh.'

The Georgian mill house and mill buildings are now buried beneath the modern meat processing plant which is part of the Goodman group. The 'meat factory' – as it was known in the local vernacular – was set up in 1968 by four local people and run by them for several years until sold.

There is good fishing on the Nenagh river for the last 14 miles of its 28-mile length. Access to the stretches is at the various bridges. The Tourist Information Offices and vendors of fishing tackle have available an information leaflet and the necessary club membership certificates for 3 days, 21 days, and the full season.

A signpost alongside the green area, in the middle of which is the 'Cuckoo's well', directs one to our next village, Puckane going firstly through the townland of Grange Upper and then into Ballyanny Upper (*baile eanaigh/a marshy area*). A noticeable feature nowadays as one drives through the Irish countryside is the number of *very* large fields – all created by the removal of the hedges, or ditches as we call them, which divide fields from each other. This practice has changed the landscape radically, both ecologically and visually.

Though new dwelling houses of various sizes and designs predominate on the route, one is heartened to see that an old dwelling has survived here and there. Watch out for these between here and Puckane.

The next landmark, about three-quarters of a mile on, is the stream and sedge-and-lily-filled mill pond (nearly dried out) to the right which supplied water to turn the under-shot wheel of the mill on the opposite side of the road. Having done its work, the water emptied into the Nenagh river at Clarianna Bridge. James Stapleton was the occupier of the mill and Robert Leeson the 'immediate lessor' in 1850 when the Primary Valuation of land and buildings was made. Subsequent owners were Thomas Clerihan and his nephew Martin. It was in operation during World War II (1940s). The mill owner's fine cut-stone house in the yard is still inhabited.

A short distance on (on the right) is a small agriculture-based industry which distributes its products, under the Agritech label, throughout all the thirty-two counties of Ireland. Agritech pioneered a powdered silage additive in 1983. This is manufactured here, as are mineral supplements for cattle. The company also blends grass seeds to different standard formulae or to a client's own prescription.

Just beyond that business premises the little bye-road to the left takes one down to Clarianna Bridge and back to Nenagh either by Rockford or Moyroe. Both these roads are immensely popular with walkers, and equally familiar to Nenagh Olympic Athletic Club runners as part of the 'Dromin Run' – both as a regular training circuit and the course for the annual John Hogan-Michael McGrath Cup.

There is a major move away from concrete blocks to real stone for walls and entrances to houses. The end result varies enormously – from finely-built dry stone walling to heavily-mortared examples. Some fine out-buildings, entrances and mills – albeit many in need of repair – have fallen victim to the revival. The first revival wall we meet on this road is fronting a renovated house which was originally built for an ex-Serviceman. There are two pairs of such houses on the Ballina route. All date from the mid-1920s, were designed by W. H. Howard, architect, and had the luxury of an outside earth closet (toilet).

Ballyanny townland was the birthplace of Archdeacon Stephen Slattery whose lifespan and tenure of service as a Catholic priest is a record for the area – his age at death in 1955 was one year short of the century and his priesthood lasted three-quarters of a century. A relation and namesake from the same townland is Bishop Hugh Slattery, M.S.C., who ministers in a diocese in South Africa.

Knigh

Opposite the new 'white house' on the right is an old-style farmhouse (with dormer windows) with the typical arrangement of out-offices close by. Evidence of such traditional farm buildings adapted to intensive farming abound on this route via slated houses, silage pits, cattle in yards, suckling calves, former hay sheds filled with polythene-wrapped silage and so on.

Our road is now on the verge of Knigh townland (*possibly cinn eich/a hill shaped like a horse's head*). Knigh graveyard, on the left and set back a bit from the road, is a typical rural burial place – the ruin of an old parish church, surrounded by a graveyard which is nearly always inter-denominational as is this one. The ruin here has no distinguishing features and is deemed to belong to the late fifteenth century. The stone work is loose and irregular and the size of the stones varies, with some particularly large. The story of its origin applies to most of the parish church ruins encountered on both routes.

Parishes, which are subdivisions of dioceses, were delineated in the twelfth century. In time each acquired its own stone church. This obtained until the division in the Christian Church in the sixteenth century brought about by the Reformation following which parish churches and property were vested in the Reformed or Anglican Church. Though some churches continued to be used for Catholic worship the clergy or congregation had no authority to maintain them and they soon fell in into disrepair. Some churches were used by the Reformed Church (later called Church of Ireland) and, as you will see at Lorrha, the old parish church was incorporated in their newer building. Meanwhile, the majority Catholic population worshipped in simple thatched Mass houses. Towards the end of the eighteenth century the Catholic Church underwent re-organisation which extended to amalgamation of two, three or more pre-Reformation parishes to create the modern Roman Catholic parish.

The erection of new parish churches followed.

The oldest inscribed stone in the graveyard here at Knigh is on the extreme right in the west/rear section of the church. It is the oft-quoted one commemorating 'Caleb Minnitt ... barbarously murdered by John Chery, Ann Parker, James McDowel and others at Crannagh ...the 2nd day of April 1707'. Caleb, not the most honourable of young men, met his death as a result of his refusal to marry his girlfriend, Ann Parker who was, in all probability, pregnant.

Knigh graveyard is the burial place of the Fogartys (some of Kilcoleman), the Wolfes and Kingsleys of Rockford, Minnitts of Annabeg and Fletchers of Shannonhall.

The next junction, Knigh Cross, has three notable features in its vicinity – a well-preserved small dwelling in traditional style, known locally as Knigh Dispensary; the monument to the two O'Briens from Nenagh who were murdered near here following their arrest during the War of Independence in November 1920; and, looking down on both, the remains of a tower house.

Tower houses were the fortified houses of substantial landowners. This one here at Knigh is probably of early sixteenth-century vintage. It was built by an O'Kennedy, the dominant Gaelic land-owning family in this area until the land confiscations of the Cromwellian period (mid-seventeenth century). Their power will be evident from the ruins of their several tower houses we will encounter on the route. The three septs of the O'Kennedys were distinguished from each other by the colour of their hair – Donn (brown), Rua (red) and Fionn (fair). Knigh was O'Kennedy Fionn territory.

The dispensary was part of the free medical care network administered successively since 1851 by the Nenagh Poor Law Union Board of Guardians, Board of Health, Tipperary (N.R.) Co. Council, and the Mid-Western Health Board. The service here commenced in 1873 and lasted until 1991 when the 'choice of doctor scheme' brought an end to such institutions.

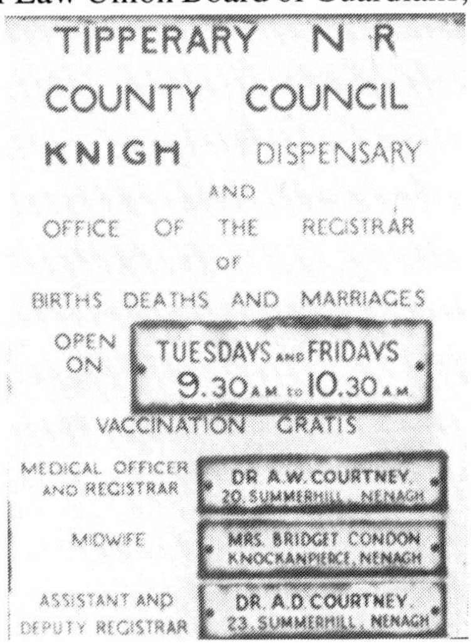

The road to the left goes across to the Nenagh-Dromineer road via Ballyartella townland, and the one to the right joins the Nenagh-Borrisokane road. However, you stay on the main road.

Just past the dispensary and near a new house is a good point to view the ring of hills.

For their names see the profiles on the opposite page.

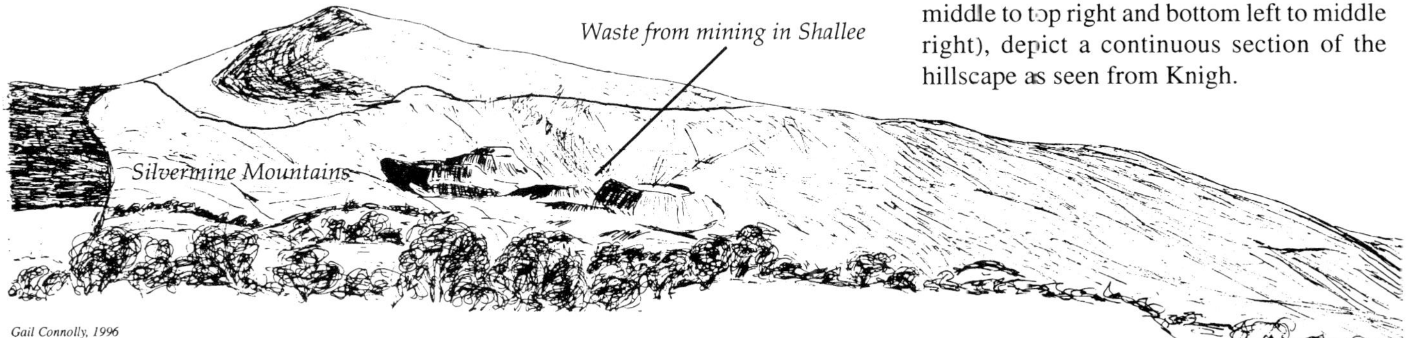

These three profiles, joined together (left middle to top right and bottom left to middle right), depict a continuous section of the hillscape as seen from Knigh.

Gail Connolly, 1996

Tountinna, and Loughtea with the Slieve Bernagh range behind, to the right of Keeper, can also be seen from Knigh; they are pictured on page 28.

Portrait of a Parish: Monsea and Killodiernan, by Daniel Grace (1996), gives substantial detail on the Minnitt and O'Brien murders and on the families buried in Knigh; it has a full chapter on the O'Kennedys and their importance hereabouts. It also catalogues the surviving field monuments to be found in the Knigh area. These include a burial cairn, a hill fort, stone forts or cahers, ring forts and a moated site. However, they are all in private ownership and accordingly not signposted or easily accessible.

This view continues – low hedges permitting – as the road, tree-lined in parts and winding, sweeps on to the extensive woodland which surrounds Lisduff House – the legacy of several generations of Minnits.

The Minnitts

The first Minnitt to settle in Knigh acquired the land by purchase in the late 1600s, and the old O'Kennedy tower house here initially sufficed as a dwelling. An eighteenth-century folly, known locally as 'the Turret', sits atop Blackfort/ Lisduff Hill (to the left). The hill is shown on the Ordnance Survey map as crowned by a two-ringed fort, with the folly standing on the raised platform within the fort. Daniel Grace describes it 'as a well-defended stone fort encircling the hill'. It was damaged during land reclamation some years ago.

For their new house the Minnitt builders selected a site at the foot of the hill and built a Georgian mansion sometime between 1770 and 1790. The house, two-storey over a basement, came into the ownership of the Minehan family in the mid-1920s; it, and the fine array of stone out-buildings, continue to be well cared for.

Puckane

It's a pleasant one-mile drive from the Lisduff House gateway to the village of Puckane (*pocán/puck goat*).

The cruciform-shaped Catholic church is on the verge of the village. Its datestone of 1859 gives the names in Latin of the builder, James Darcy, the parish priest, Eugene Malone, and the Bishop of the time, Dr Michael Flannery.

Behind the altar is a stained glass window from the Harry Clarke Studio, Dublin, with panels depicting the Crucifixion and Ascension. It was donated in 1934 by Josephine Chase, née Minehan and a native of the parish, domiciled in New York.

Harry Clarke (1889-1931) was a Dublin-based illustrator and stained glass artist. A few years ago the window was taken down, cleaned and re-leaded. Also worthy of note are the windows in the side aisles depicting the Last Supper and the Finding of Jesus in the Temple. Windows from the Clarke studio can also be seen on the Ballina-Killaloe route and there is a really magnificent Clarke window in Cloughjordan R.C. church, 12 miles (19km) from Borrisokane.

Just up the narrow road to the left is an early national school now utilised as a builder's office. It was obviously an elegant building in its day – again, Portrait *of a Parish: Monsea and Killodiernan* has its story in some detail.

The village and outskirts has houses built by Tipperary (N.R.) Co. Council, the Rural Housing Organisation, the Rent-an-Irish Cottage scheme, and private enterprise. Most of the village's older houses were thatched at one time and two near the Lourdes Grotto still retain that form of roofing.

The Grotto (1957) has stones from three Marian apparition sites, Fatima, Lourdes and Knock, incorporated in the stonework. The signposts nearby direct us to Coolbawn 4 miles (6.4km) and L. Derg Drive/Bóthar an Locha.

O'Kennedy Country

This is very much O'Kennedy country. Here in Puckane the Kennedy business has its date of establishment and the O'Kennedy coat of arms on the signboard. Jimmy Kennedy is a native son – the first of the modern prolific-scoring hurlers, notably during Tipperary's All-Ireland hat-trick, 1949-51. His daughter, Louise Kennedy, is an internationally-acclaimed fashion designer.

The Rent-an-Irish-Cottage scheme has twelve houses and are rarely without tenants. This scheme, funded by community and semi-State investment, was built in two phases in the early 1970s. The comeback of the craft of thatching is very much in evidence here. The majority of the houses are thatched with reeds and the latest programme has included an additional thatched cap with the scollops applied in a decorative way. When applied first the thatch is golden coloured but this weathers to an attractive grey-brown.

As well as providing accommodation for holidaymakers the scheme provides convenient temporary residences for persons awaiting the completion of a new house or between the sale of a business or house and acquisition of another. The cottage idea was the brain-child of a Shannon Development executive and similar schemes are to be found in Holycross and Terryglass in Co. Tipperary and in Co. Clare. However, all schemes were sold out of community and Shannon Development ownership a few years ago.

A short stretch of tree-lined road brings one past the entrances to Lodge and Rockvalley on the right. The parish's former Glebe (residence of the Church of Ireland Rector) is down an avenue on the left close to Killodiernan Church of Ireland church with its typical square tower. The church was built in 1811 but underwent repairs and additions – the chancel/altar area and vestry – in the 1870s. Only members of the Church of Ireland are buried in the graveyard. The gravestone inscriptions are of immense interest as they record for the social historian and genealogist key information on landed families in the parish – Waller, Holmes, Minnitt, Galway, Studdert, Woodward, Headech.

The fine three-arched entrance gate to Peterfield/Johnstown House, and its gate lodge, nestle in the bend of the road. The gate probably dates from the 1770s when the Big House (now demolished) was built by Peter Holmes, ancestor of the man for whom Peter Street in Nenagh was named. The main avenue to the house skirted past Poulawee, one of several small lakes in this area.

The lodge, a dwelling for most of its life, has been rehabilitated and given the Gaelic name of 'Teach an Gheata' (the gatehouse). Beside this is Puckane Crafts founded in 1971. Here they make quality 3-D and plain fretwork plaques of which a considerable proportion is exported to the United States of America. It is now owned by Paddy and Alice Walsh, and trades as Walshcraft. The gate lodge is its retail outlet.

Killodiernan Church

A signpost beside the lodge points to Killodiernan old parish church which has decorated columns inserted in a Hiberno-Romanesque doorway (*cill Ó dTiarnáin/the church of the Ó Tiernans*). It is pleasantly sited with good views of Poulawee and Lough Derg.

Writing in the diocesan journal *Molua,* Dermot F. Gleeson said of the ruin:

> It was originally a typical smaller twelfth-century Celtic Romanesque erection. The west door has unfortunately been burst open by tree roots and is now filled up with stones. It is possible to make out the twelfth-century arches in sandstone but the stone filling prevents any proper examination. The East window, also twelfth century, cannot be properly seen on account of growths ... The church like many others was partly re-edified in the fifteenth century. (1951)
>
> The west door has been reconstructed in so far as possible, the walls have been cleaned and the whole fabric pointed. (1955)

Peter Harbison, in his *Guide to National Monuments of Ireland*, mentions the 'scroll work and spirals' on 'the door which was presumably taken from an earlier church on the site and built into the later medieval church ... Some of the stones of the doorway have, however been wrongly fitted in the course of reconstruction.'

The ruin fell into a dangerous state of repair again in the 1980s and this time local initiative and a scheme under the auspices of FÁS (the national training authority) did a considerable amount of repair and conservation work. However, the wrongly fitted stones referred to above were not corrected. The north-east gable (to your right as you come in) has a small mortuary chapel attached. This is the burial place of Dr Denis Harty, vicar apostolic of the diocese of Killaloe in the mid-seventeenth century. The Latin inscription on the flat slab gives its date as 1667.

Clareen & Claree Loughs

The road swings sharp right at Teach an Gheata and along by Clareen Lough which lies behind the hedge on the right (*cláirín/a little level area*). The lough is about one third of a mile long and lies parallel to the road.

Looking across the lake one can see the white-gabled front of Lodge. The house figures in Brian de Breffny and Rosemary ffolliott's *Houses of Ireland*. They thought the central section of the house might well have been a farmhouse from the Williamite period (1690s) and quoted an unverified tradition that it was built by a chaplain in King William III's (William of Orange) army. But Daniel Grace in researching his parish history found it to date from circa 1700 and to have been built by the son of a Cromwellian grantee, one Samuel Barry. Two gabled wings, with Venetian windows, were added in the 1770s.

At the next T-junction Claree Lough is visible in the fields ahead. It is an irregularly-shaped lake extending in a north-south direction about half a mile long. The plant and animal life in Poulawee, Clareen and Claree lake fens (low marshy land covered with water) is classified as of 'local importance' in a Foras Forbartha survey done for the county some years ago and incorporated in the North Riding's current Development Plan.

Our route follows the 'Coolbawn 3 miles' sign along a winding road through the townland of Knocknacartan, more frequently called Claree. One needs to drive or cycle carefully as there are some tricky bends.

Ballycolliton

A nice one-arched bridge straddles the Ballycolliton river heading westwards for Lough Derg. Have a quiet smile at the proximity of the 'community alert' and 'beware of the bull' signs and the position of the latter. The fields hereabouts are usually mottled with sheep.

To your right is another O'Kennedy tower house. In *The Last Lords of Ormond* Dr Dermot F. Gleeson gives a list of persons killed at a battle in Ballycolliton on 30 September 1598/9 during the rebellion led by the Earl of Tyrone. Among the O'Kennedys killed were Owney of Ballicolliton and Dermot of Knigh.

The tower house here at Ballycolliton is incorporated into the out-buildings of the later Cleburne owners – descendants of William Cleburne who purchased the land from a Cromwellian grantee, Captain Solomon Cambie. The Cleburne house has since been replaced. We will come across the burial place of the Cleburnes farther on.

A short distance on, a signpost for Luska (loisgthe/burnt ground) invites one down the first of many little roads one meets and which lead to Lough Derg's edge where you can enjoy an extensive and scenic view of the lake.

The terrain to the left is interesting, small mounds covered with a mix of hazel, alder, holly and furze/gorse overlooking the Ballycolliton river valley. Tountinna and Loughtea hills seem to be at the end of the road. The ivy-covered remains of Annagh tower house, standing sentinel on the hill, will already have caught your eye – looking like the square-shouldered man with a tall hat in the Sandeman Port advertisement. It is a landmark for both sailors and landlubbers.

Though it looks intact from the roadside the wall on the other side is more or less gone. Accordingly, its architectural innards can be seen from ground level close up.

It too was probably built by an O'Kennedy but acquired later by an O'Hurley who was in possession in 1654. He lost land and home to Solomon Cambie. Cambie subsequently sold it to Minchins circa 1699. Later Minchins moved down from their look-out tower on the exposed hill and built a plain, solid two-storey L-shaped house, with slated gable and marvellous chimney stacks, about half-way down the hill. In time it too was vacated; sadly, it was demolished in 1989.

Shortly after passing the modern bungalow, sited in front of the demolished house, the road swings right and so passes very close to the tower house. At that point there is another small lake – Annagh – on the left.

Nature Abundant

In Lough Derg itself the growth of reeds, rushes and long grasses provides food and shelter for families of mute swans, ducks and waterhens/moorhens. The waters around the shore have some treacherous rocks but locals know the channels through which to bring their boats into safe mooring points.

Here also you may find the wild flower Inula Salicina/Irish Fleabane, identifiable by its neat golden daisy-like flowers on long stems (see back cover). According to the *Red Data Book*, published by the Wildlife Service in 1988, this plant is confined to the shores of Lough Derg and, though found throughout Europe, is not found anywhere else in what used to be called the British Isles.

The expanse of land in the water in front of you is Cameron Island. It lies in the parish of Kilbarron and can be approached by a causeway. It is about half a mile long. Its 60 acres of grazing land were valued at £30 in the Primary Valuation of 1850. John Minchin was the owner with John Tuohy and Patrick Houlihan tenants of the land while Stephen Murphy was the occupier of the island's only house valued at 15*s*. (75p). The island does not have regular inhabitants now, only a holiday home or two. Islandbrien, a wild bird sanctuary, lies to the south-west/left of Cameron.

The narrow road (a cul-de-sac) by the water's edge goes past Luska House which is a good example of a Victorian villa, to the quayside corn store tastefully and imaginatively converted to a dwelling by its Waller owner in the 1930s. The latter dwelling fetched well over £100,000 when sold in the mid-1990s.

One now has a choice of continuing along by the lakeshore through the townlands of Glenbower and Skehanagh to Kilbarron/Skehanagh quay on an old but upgraded road, or of returning back to the main road and continuing on to Coolbawn Post Office and then turning left for the quay. The origins of the placenames are, respectively: *gleann bodhar/*a *deaf glen – indicating a glen with an echo similar to the loud speech of a deaf person; cill Bhairfhionn/ St Barrin's church; cúil bán/a whitish corner.*

For the purpose of this guide we'll first take the lakeshore route by swinging left at the Coolbawn sign beside an eye-catching house and garden. The road now goes behind the east end of Cameron and on to a developed viewing point with a children's play area beside placid water and a small quay. In the summer the roadside verge here is virtually a herbaceous border of wild flowers. Heather, cow parsley, vetches, wild rose, field scabious and hardheads and even that rare inula salicina/Irish fleabane can be spotted.

A short, pleasant drive brings one to Kilbarron/Skehanagh quay. This is an oasis of peace, with rushes and water-hens a-plenty. Cameron now lies to the left with Keeper Hill visible behind it. The distant summits of Tountinna and Loughtea, in profile, are easily identified (they lie above the village of Portroe which is on the Nenagh to Ballina-Killaloe route) while Co. Clare's Slieve Bernagh and Co. Galway's Slieve Aughty are on the horizon.

The Largest Island

The largest of Lough Derg's islands, Illaunmore/Islandmore with its 225 acres, lies about one mile off the Tipperary shore but in Co. Clare. There were four families living on it at one time. They enjoyed their own national school between 1900 and 1917 – it's still there on the north-west corner. Nowadays, the privately-owned island is utilised for farming, and pheasant farming for commercial shoots, with related residences and a holiday home.

Islandmore has a different soil to the other islands in its vicinity – it is arable land suitable for grain crops like wheat and barley, while the other islands are mostly sand and have only about six inches of soil on the surface.

The names Tiernan and O'Meara are closely associated with the island's history. The boundaries of Counties Clare, Tipperary and Galway meet north of it.

The late Dermot F. Gleeson saw, and later described in writing, two seventh or eighth-century cross slabs in the precincts of the old church ruin on the north-east corner of the island in 1955. There was also a standing stone a

short distance away. One of the slabs (right) appears to be similar to those dug up in Latteragh graveyard a few years ago and now on display in Nenagh District Heritage Centre. Latteragh, off the Nenagh-Thurles road, was the site of a monastery founded by St. Odran who died circa AD 574.

It is well worth taking time off to walk up the road opposite the quay and enjoy the panoramic view of the islands and the lake generally.

The red-brick building beside that road is the intake treatment plant of a regional water scheme, using lake water, under construction by Tipperary (N.R.) County Council.

On the move again, the main road swings away from the water after a short distance. The next notable landmark is Kilbarron graveyard on the right at a bend in the road. As at Knigh, this burial ground surrounds the ruin of the old parish church.

The ruin is of a substantial church 22 feet (35m long), loosely constructed of stones of different types among which are limestone and red sandstone; some are exceptionally large. Its windows are, in general, in a good state of preservation externally though very damaged on the inside.

Two Cleburnes of Ballycolliton who died in the seventeenth century are buried here: Elizabeth, all of thirteen days old who died in 1682, and William, gentleman, who died two years later. They are commemorated by a plaque and large tomb, respectively.

In the recent clean-up of the ruin a flat stone marking the grave of Rev. Donatus Kennedy (died 1706) was uncovered to the right of the Cleburne vault.

Muintir Uí Cinnéide

Ireland's struggle for independence is recalled in the gravestone which commemorates Micheál Ó Cinnéide, Nenagh, aged 27 years, who died approximately four weeks after being wounded in the attack by Tipperary No. 1 Brigade of the I(rish R(epublican) A(rmy) on Borrisokane R(oyal I(rish) C(onstabulary) barracks in June 1920.

As one approaches the main road a fine dwelling in the wood to the right catches the eye. It was a Protestant school in the last century and has been refurbished.

The entrance gates and uninhabited but stylish gate lodge of Castletown House, formerly called Castle Cambie, is on the left. The chimney stacks and gables of the Big House, as seen from the main road, belie the fact that it is actually a sixteenth-century tower house adapted to twentieth-century standards – which include a commodious nineteenth-century extension in tower house style. This too was O'Kennedy property up to the mid-seventeenth-century confiscations. The first Cromwellian grantee soon sold it on to Captain Solomon Cambie whom we met in relation to Ballycolliton and Annagh. Descendants of Solomon still live in North Tipperary though not in this area. One was John Henry Cambie (born 1836) who emigrated to Canada and became an eminent engineer there.

If, instead of taking that lakeshore drive, you had opted to return from Luska to the main road, it was a mile-long stretch to Coolbawn Cross where the lakeshore road re-joins it.

Glimpses of Annagh tower house and the third Minchin residence, 'Annagh Lodge', backed by extensive woods, can be seen to the left on your way. Long gone from Minchin ownership, it is now a guesthouse.

A short distance on, tower house spotters will notice the square one of Lisquillibeen a few fields in to the right – it's clearly visible at a gateway a hundred metres/yards before a house alongside which is the access road. However, it is privately owned and should not be explored without the land owner's permission.

The tower house is strategically sited on top of a rocky hillock which is surrounded by boggy land. It is in a very good state of preservation with loops, corbels, slop stones and garderobe chute (lavatory) intact. Rory and William Kennedy of Brockagh and John Kennedy of Knigh were among the seventeenth-century owners of Lisquillibeen townland (*lios coill an beann/ the fort on the hazel-covered steep hill*).

The best view from the road is near a large tree on the right, a little bit up the incline past the entrance (see photograph on page 45).

Lisquillibeen was the birthplace of James Francis Hogan (1854-1924), teacher journalist, author and politician, who emigrated to Australia with his parents in early childhood. An entry for him in the Australian Directory of Biography details his varied career. He wrote several books including *The Irish in Australia* (1887). Later he came to live in London and in 1893 was nominated and returned unopposed to represent Mid Tipperary in the British House of Commons – a position he held until 1900. He spent his final years in London working as a journalist.

The road we are traversing runs through open country (where tillage abounds) for a short while before the trees surrounding Kilbarron Church of Ireland parish church appear ahead on the left. The entrance gate, backed by an overgrown, boreen-like avenue, is on the left at a bend on the road. The church was built in 1822 and de-consecrated in 1975. Happily, it may soon be refurbished as a dwelling, having fetched the princely sum of £40,000 in 1992. The purchaser was Patrick Bergin, the film actor of *Sleeping with the*

Enemy fame.

The adjoining graveyard is the burial place of many of the lakeside families prominent in the area for several generations, notably Minchins, Bruces, Towers and Biggs.

A wall tablet in the church recorded the tragic heroism of a native son, Frederic F. R. Minchin, Annagh, 'who perished on the first attempt ever to fly the Atlantic from England to America' in September 1927. The memorial is now in the Heritage Centre in Nenagh; a full account of this fateful event will appear in a history of this area now being prepared for publication.

The general shop at Coolbawn Cross houses the post office. Shannonside Language Centre, recognised by the Department of Education for the teaching of English as a foreign language, is also located hereabouts. Students can opt for accommodation in a local country hotel, rented cottage or in residence with a local family. The teachers travel to them. A combination of language course plus horse riding or sailing or painting is also on offer.

The road to the right leads to the village of Kilbarron which has a church, school, community hall, a public house, and a pitch-and-putt course.

In summer the little vacant house beside the pump is covered with fuschia. Houses of this size and design are fast disappearing from town and country. This one, built of rubble stone, was a two-roomed dwelling. Its chimney breast, with crude, unplaned supporting beam is intact as are the lintels over the doors and windows.

Parklands

If you had decided not to detour to the water's edge at Luska your first view of Lough Derg and its backdrop of hills is just past Coolbawn Cross. Here at a bend on the road Islandmore, and quite a wide expanse of water, form a background as one looks down on the park land which surrounds Castletown House.

Beech and sycamore trees line the approach to Lesseragh House, sited below the level of the road on the left. This house was built in the 1870s by Major William Bruce. The townland is O'Meara's Acres and the previous house which stood on or near the site of the present one was called 'Mungo Park' – more likely to have been so named due to a mistranslation of the adjoining townland of Gortmungo than for Mungo Park (1771-1806), the Scottish explorer of the River Niger source. On the 1840 O.S. sheet 'Mungo Park' is on the right of a low-lying road but this was re-routed later to a higher level.

It is a pleasant drive now, past the entrance to Curraghmore House (now in ruins). Bellevue townland straddles the road for some of the way. A single tree guards the entrance to Bellevue House (inhabited), whose woodland is termed of 'regional interest' in the North Riding's County Development Plan.

The road runs downhill now as it swings away from the lake, through the fragmented townland of Scriboge on the left, then through Ballyscanlon on the right and Mota on the left.

The area is spotted with fine new houses built on elevated sites to get full value of the view. Central heating and triple glazing have made all this possible. One notes that older houses, inhabited or abandoned, favoured the lower ground.

On the left the entrance to Brookfield House (inhabited) is also guarded by a tree. Just past the house with a galvanised roof is an obviously new road heading off in the direction of the lake. This leads to what is shown on the maps as 'Belvedere Quay' but is in fact a raised look-out. A leisure development mooted for there in 1992 was re-activated in 1996.

The roads, countryside and lake was familiar territory to Paddy Tierney (1904-90), who served as TD (Teachta Dála/member of Dáil Éireann or parliament) for North Tipperary, 1957-69, and Senator, 1954-7. Small in stature, large in character, he was a man of ready wit. During an interview on radio after his retirement from politics, he was asked how he divided his time between his occupation of farming and his hobby, fishing on Lough Derg. He responded, 'Well, God made the world ninety per cent water and ten per cent land, and I follow his example'.

The road is tree-lined for a while before the Mota Quay signpost and another recommended detour.

The Two Quays: Two Short Detours

This approach road to the lake has the best view so far. At the water's edge there is an open area with seats and good perspectives for artists and photographers. The Co. Galway shoreline,1.5 miles (2.4 km) distant, dominates the view ahead. There is a good growth of rushes for the would-be basket-maker.

Back to the main road again.

Another mile of driving takes one past the trees screening Kilgarvan House, to the signpost for the quay of the same name.

The spur to the quayside is just half a mile long.

It has an antique shop and the Brocka-on-the-Water restaurant, which received praise in the *Bridgestone Irish Food Guide*. There is a location map of attractions in the area, sited beside the water, plus toilets, seats, car park and space for tents. But the quay's primary function is as a developed harbour for boats – the first one up-lake from Dromineer on the Tipperary side.

The quay is also the headquarters of Kilgarvan Anglers Association. Members can do repairs and general maintenance on their craft in their fine club-house – visiting boats in distress are also facilitated.

There are trout, pike, perch and bream to be caught by fisherfolk. The Association organises an April-to-October competition for the heaviest fish caught by an overseas visitor. For the land-bound there is a new view again with Foot's Island just offshore, swans, reeds and rushes, boats coming and going and marvellous sunsets – all great subjects for photographers and video/ cine enthusiasts. A notice reminds fisherfolk:

HELP THE PIKE SURVIVE PUT IT BACK ALIVE
DEN HECHT NICHT DEFAHRDEN IMMER ZURUCKWERFEN
POUR QUE VIVE LE BROCHET FAUT LE REJETER

Return to the main road again for the mile-long run to Ballinderry.

The craft of building dry-stone walls is evident in divisions between the fields on the left-hand side of the road and indeed as the field and road boundary in some stretches.

Drominagh's Bridge and Trees

At Ballinderry the traveller has a choice of two roads to Terryglass (*tír dhá ghlas/the territory of the two streams; a seventh-century Life of St. Colum translates it literally into Latin: ager duorum rivorum).* The older one is to the left (at the sign pointing to Gurthalougha). It goes over quaint Drominagh Bridge which straddles the Ballyfinboy river (about 3 mins drive).

Just short of the bridge is the entrance to Gurthalougha House which stands at the lake's edge. As it is now a guesthouse (in the Hidden Ireland group) visitors have access to the extensive woodland and lakeside walks. It is a paradise for nature trailers and outdoor enthusiasts.

The Ballyfinboy river (*baile finn mhaigh/the place [on] the fair plain*) separates Gurthalougha and Drominagh. The bridge here is a notable landmark with its two covered recesses – for the collection of tolls, it is thought. The datestone over the recess on the right proclaims Richard Biggs to have been the overseer for its construction in 1776.

The landscape, personalities, lifestyles and the

amenities of Drominagh (*druimneach/ridged land*), Ballinderry (*baile an doire/the town or area of the oak wood*), and this corner of North Tipperary generally in the 1930s, have been preserved in the late Pamela Hinkson's book, *Irish Gold.* Miss Hinkson, a daughter of Katherine Tynan the poet, was a friend of the Esmondes of Drominagh House and spent long holidays there. In her book she called it, 'Golden Wood'.

Drominagh House is screened from view by fine trees, an attractive gate lodge stands near the entrance. Donagh Kennedy of Lackeen was the owner hereabouts in the mid-seventeenth century. Two hundred years on Edward Biggs was the occupier; the Esmondes came later again – in the late 1800s. The 'O'Kennedy's old ruined castle' – so described in 1654 – is still standing though badly damaged by frost a decade or so ago.

Castletown, Bellevue, Mota, Kilgarvan, Gurthalougha, and Drominagh are typical of the legacy of Big Houses to be found close to the lakeshore all the way from Ballina-Killaloe to Portumna Bridge. Many were built by direct descendants of the settlers of the Cromwellian era and are an intrinsic part of the social history of the area.

The road to Terryglass is to the left at the T-junction a short distance on.

This is tree country. About a third of a mile down to the right is Drominagh Lodge, a small Georgian house built within a ring fort on which there is a fine crop of mature beech trees. Here farmer Matt Fogarty has developed what began as a hobby in the 1950s into a thriving and fulfilling family business. His hardwood tree nursery extends over twenty-eight acres, carrying over two hundred and thirty different species, including the giant redwood, tulip and walnut trees. Visitors are welcome but an appointment is advisable. The nursery has an annual Open Day in mid-July under the auspices of the national tree support group, Crann (the Irish word for tree and pronounced 'crown').

On the way to Terryglass there are occasional glimpses of the lake, which is never farther than a mile cross-country. For decades the apple orchards of Kylenoe, on the right, enjoyed a high reputation countrywide. However, the orchard acreage has been greatly reduced in recent years. Thomas Downey, well-known to purchasers of their 'Golden Delicious' and other brands, received a Royal Dublin Society Award for his fifty years of service here as an horticultural assistant. Though now retired the orchards still enjoy the benefit of his immense knowledge and expertise.

The grassland and woodland at Gortmore point – the tip of a peninsula – away to one's left, are categorised as of 'national importance' in the Development Plan already referred to.

The road runs very near the lake shoreline as it enters the townland of Terryglass. This approach road to the village, with neat houses and new stone walls, equals that from Portumna.

Ballinderry For All Seasons

Before describing Terryglass it's best to document the features on the outskirts of Ballinderry and on the main road which links the two villages.

Ballinderry village has a cluster of neat dwellings and businesses, trees, and a river – the Ballyfinboy that one meets at Drominagh Bridge. The grass verge with picnic tables, just beyond the bye-road to Terryglass via Drominagh, is a good point from which to view the old corn mill and distillery. The massive mill wheel is intact as is a considerable amount of the mill's internal features. However, one should seek the owner's permission before dashing off on a grand tour. This is one of two mills on the Ballyfinboy river, the other being at Borrisokane.

The signpost at the T-junction points left to Terryglass. The stone bridge here has four arches. Just over the bridge and beside the river is the cutest little house on the route – a whitewashed cottage of 'cabin' proportions.

Ballinderry scores high points in the annual Tidy Towns competition. Village life, as it was in the 1930s, is beautifully portrayed in Pamela Hinkson's *Irish Gold.* Miss Hinkson, 'a passionate letter writer and receiver', was a frequent customer of the post office here. She devoted a whole chapter of her book to it and sang the praises of the three Miss Kennedys who ran it.

> It is the most beautiful of all the whitewashed cottages in Ireland, and I stand by that statement. There is a little yard with the tidy stone wall edging it. ... You enter the Post Office by the living-room-kitchen. Here is a perfect interior. I sometimes think of it when I am in London, walking perhaps in a street of tall houses, with a glimpse through the windows of sad people dining at hotel dining tables.

A fairly recent addition to village life has been the small industry of Lakeshore Foods founded by Hilary Henry in 1986. It has manufactured a variety of mustards from the beginning and have added dressings, a sauce, a glaze, and other products now numbering twenty-two in all. Specialised items are produced for own-label companies in Ireland and the U.K. Twenty percent of Lakeshore Foods goes overseas, including to the USA and South Africa. This 'small cottage industry' and the adjoining summer season tea rooms have won commendation in the *Bridgestone Irish Food Guide.*

A fine Georgian house, set back from the road on the left, catches the eye. The road now continues on past a public house with a serviced caravan park and then by a garage business built up by the man who was 'the little barefoot figure, wrapped in oilskins' whom Miss Hinkson encountered on a very wet day and gave a lift to when he was on his way to the post office to collect his grandfather's pension – an encounter which is also related in *Irish Gold.* Her post office is no more.

The redundant stone quarry is one of the features which catch the eye as one takes the pleasant, two-and-a-half mile downhill run to Terryglass. The quarrying of limestone, gritstone and sandstone for road-making and building purposes has left a great legacy of exposed rock profiles throughout the county. These cut-away quarries are worth examining if one's interest lies in geology or botany.

Tidiest Terryglass

Terryglass's church spire soon looms ahead. The village's selection as the Tidiest Town in Ireland in 1983 and the attendant publicity were echoes of the fame which the area enjoyed when St. Colum's monastery and place of learning was of great importance from AD 548 to 1148. One of Ireland's national treasures, the Book of Leinster (now in Trinity College library), was probably compiled here sometime between AD 1151 and 1225.

The village's advantageous location on the River Shannon today was detrimental to it when it was a monastic settlement. The great waterway brought the Viking raiders right to the door and records show that it was plundered and burnt on six occasions between AD 805 and 1164.

In contrast to what one finds further along the route at Lorrha, where medieval monastic settlements followed on the Early Christian one and where substantial remains from that era survive, Terryglass's monastic glory ended with the destruction of the Early Christian foundation.

No traces remain of the monastic enclosure other than a slight outline east of the village which showed up in an aerial photograph some years ago. Of the two later medieval buildings – fourteenth-century parish church and sixteenth-century tower house and bawn – only scant remains survive. A partial wall of the church survives in the graveyard, while an oblong courtyard (with three of its four curtain walls remaining) and a gateway of the tower house can be seen near Paddy's Bar.

Paddy's sports its '7 Day Licence for the sale of Beers & Spirits for consumption on the premises' over the door. It has a high reputation for bar food as well as thirst quenchers. The Derg Inn alongside has acquired an equivalent culinary reputation. An American voice, at an outdoor table in the sunshine, recently proffered the information that one of the establishments had 'the best milkshakes in Ireland'.

The short street is regularly alive with the gift of many tongues: during the trip which produced the photographs on page 47, an enquiry identified German, Dutch and Danish, as well as the English language from Somerset in England, Miami in USA, and that spoken by Irish people returned on holidays – a category specified by themselves and notable generally as a strong component of inward tourism.

The Protestant church, dating from circa 1838, was given a new lease of life in the 1980s when it underwent a tasteful conversion to residence and craft-workshop. Under the management of well-known artist Jenny Boelens it now functions as craft shop and gallery and carries a fine stock of Irish-made goods – some rare and unusual like the wood sculptures and bonsai, both produced locally.

A bonus for patrons of the craft shop is the cottage garden one must pass through. The air is rich with the scent of lavender, carnations and roses while a corner seat invites one to rest awhile and savour it all.

On the 1840 Ordnance Sheet the settlement of Terryglass is confined to a small area west of the bridge. It has grown extensively in recent years. The old early eighteenth-century Catholic chapel is now a community centre, having also served as a school in its time. The external wall of this focal point sports the bronze plaque recording the village's achievement in the Tidy Towns Competition of 1983.

The orchard alongside the community centre is the setting for a Sunday afternoon country market where one can buy the produce of local craftworkers as well as kitchen produce.

To the Quay

Modern dwellings, including an all-slated Rent-an-Irish Cottage scheme, have sprung up along the road to Terryglass quay. At the quayside there is a short lakeside walk, children's play area, seats for lake-viewers, toilets, facilities for swimmers and, of course, for boats. Swans and water-hens abound and there are wild flowers a-plenty – poppies, hardheads, marsh marigold, and rosebay willowherb.

The waters yield perch and pike to the fisherman.

Here too is St. Augh's Well whose spring waters are said to cure sore eyes. The ritual included a set number of prayers as the pilgrim walked around the perimeter of the well.

A bust of John Weaving (died 1987), to whom editor Ruth Delany dedicated the 1993 *Shell Guide to the River Shannon*, faces out towards the water from the small green area near the new jetty.

Looking up-lake the fine plantation of trees belong to Slevoir House, beside another little bay that is hidden from view here at Terryglass Bay. Across the lake is Portumna Castle and Forest Park.

Down lake from the quay is Old Court Castle, sited on elevated ground close to the water's edge. It is a legacy of Norman colonisation in these parts. The fourteenth-century description of it as 'a solid base of one castle with four towers of the height of 12 feet (3.6m) still applies today. Some archaeologists are of the opinion that it is an unfinished building and was never any higher. It may have been built by a Norman named John Marshal who was granted land in Terryglass. However, the de Burgo name, majority landowners across the bay in Co. Galway, appears on a document relating to the manor of Terryglass as early as 1289.

Though it is a national monument, it is privately owned and in close proximity to the owner's dwelling so would-be viewers should walk (rather than drive or cycle) down the avenue. It is not accessible from the amenity area.

After the detour to the amenity area and other attractions return to the main road and turn left over the bridge. The house on the corner is beautifully maintained in 'olde worlde' style. This was home to Harold Kent, who designed several farm implements, including a root gapper, and an automatic pig feeder for which he won a Royal Dublin Society silver medal in 1924.

The change in farming styles is reflected by the conversion of the farm hayshed, made redundant by silage making, to that of boat house.

The choice of holiday accommodation in the Terryglass area can be gauged by the presence of two signs for guesthouses at the bye-road to the right – Riverrun near the cross, and Tír na Fiúise 2km away and which is part of a working farm.

As part of the Tidy Towns prize the overall winner is presented with a piece of sculpture (chosen by themselves). The Terryglass choice – granite pillars topped by a heron – graces the grass verge on the road between the bridge and the Catholic church.

The Hickie Church

Terryglass's cruciform church in gothic style occupies a spacious site at the top of the incline. The church was built through the patronage of Lucilia Larios y Tashara Hickie, the Spanish-born wife of Colonel James Francis Hickie, Slevoir House. She was suffering from an incurable illness and died aged 45 years in 1880, the year in which the foundation stone was laid. Her husband continued the patronage until its completion. Later he undertook to finance the building of a tower and spire. Though this had not come to fruition before his death in 1913, his son, Manuel Hickie, carried out his wishes and brought it to completion in 1929.

The interior of the church has rich marble columns, marble and bronze plaques, and brass fittings not usually found in rural churches. Happily all these were retained and burnished in the interior decoration scheme undertaken in 1980-1 – the only major alteration was the removal of the altar rails and the insertion of a new altar on a raised platform to comply with the liturgical requirements of Vatican ll.

A plaque under the fourteenth station of the cross commemorates Eugene Esmonde, V.C., D.S.O., R.N., of Drominagh House, killed in action in February 1942, aged 33 years. Lt.-Commander Esmonde is the subject of a biography by Chaz Bowers (London, 1983). It contains quite a bit about

Drominagh and the Esmondes generally who included a previous winner of the Victoria Cross and two members of parliament. The Esmondes were among many Irish landed families of the time whose schooling was partly in Ireland and partly in England and who combined public service specifically for Ireland with military service for the British Empire.

Eugene Esmonde originally joined the Royal Air Force and was a squadron commander in the Fleet Air Arm of the Royal Navy when he was killed in February 1942. That occurred during an attack on a formidable German naval force in the Straits of Dover.

There is a relic of the True Cross preserved here in a specially-designed side chapel. The relic was donated by James Francis Hickie, Lieut.-Col. Royal Fusiliers, who died in February 1913, aged 79 years. The relic was verified as genuine by Pope Pius IX in June 1863.

The framed memorial card display on the rear wall of this little chapel is of immense historical and genealogical value.

The style of the adjacent graveyard, whose limestone headstones are of uniform height and in regular rows, is rare. One of the Hickie plots includes the grave of master stonemason Daniel Mohilly, Nenagh, who worked on the tower. Daniel, a native of Cork, came to Nenagh in 1892 to work on the building of St. Mary's of the Rosary church.

Carrigahorig

One enjoys occasional glimpses of Slevoir Bay on the two-mile stretch between the church and Carrigahorig. Two houses which catch the eye are the former Terryglass Glebe, now Killeen House (on the right), and the Deasy home farther on in Firmount. This attractive long house, with dormer windows, is picturesquely set against a lake backdrop; note the nice stone stile alongside the entrance.

Looking to the right you can see the distant Slieve Bloom mountains and the nearer Knockshegowna hill.

The road goes left at the next T-junction, past a pub with a thatched section of roof and through the village of Carrigahorig (*carraig an chomhraic/the hill of the confluence of two rivers*). There is also another pub, a post office and a gurgling river; another stream joins it before the bridge. The river once powered a fine corn mill called 'Santa Cruise'. Alas, it is no more, having been totally demolished and the stone sold in 1994.

Rev. Michael H. Pathe, C.Ss.R., based in Wisconsin, USA, revisited his native village in 1929 and wrote lyrically in *A Summer in Ireland* :

> Back to Carrigahorig. In that river, at the foot of the hill we played. It was our barefoot trail. We caught the speckled trout, we trapped the wild ducks here. On the old bridge we were wont to gather when the

> day's work was done – to hear a song or whisper the dark plot for a raid on an orchard, or some prank to torment a neighbour. By Joyce's barn, on the road-side, we danced in the sweet evenings of summer. Against the side of the Bridge House we fought our handball tournaments. From Flynns to Houghs we showed our prowess in cycling. In Donoghue's Mill we tramped the drying corn. Under the bridge we 'probed' for eels, or hid from an angry parent.

There is a sign to the right for Gurteen Agricultural College. Here residential students of both sexes and all denominations learn modern farming methods. The college, which was founded by the Methodist Congregation in 1947, also has conference facilities, self-catering holiday apartments, and hosts the likes of a Euro Pony Camp. Another fingerpost points to Aglishcloghane whose Ballycormac House figures in the *Bridgestone Irish Food Guide* with high praise for the 'fabulous cooks'.

A detour is recommended (5 mins drive) to the village of Lorrha (lobhar/ leper – may be from St. Finan's affliction with leprosy; he was a native of this area).

To Lorrha's 'Famed Monastic Walls'

In the midst of buildings characteristic of a typical Irish village, plus a new community hall, is a fine collection of ancient monuments which relate to the Early Christian, Norman and medieval periods.

The first to catch the eye are the church ruins of the Dominican foundation which flourished here from the 1260s by Richard de Burgo/Burke, until the end of the 1600s. Within the ruin are decorated MacEgan and O'Kennedy tombs (right) which are over three and a half centuries old and signed by their makers, Patrick Kerin and Nicholas Cowly, respectively. The work of those master craftsmen can be seen throughout South Tipperary and Co. Kilkenny.

The nearby parish church was built in 1812 and renovated in 1977 to comply with Vatican II liturgical requirements. Under the direction of the then parish priest, Very Rev. Martin Ryan, symbols of Lorrha's historic past were incorporated into the new layout. The panels of the Stowe Missal shrine were photographed, enlarged and copied in bronze to form the tabernacle door. The missal (called Stowe after the Buckinghamshire town where it was held for some time) is a ninth-century illuminated vellum manuscript probably written in Lorrha. The inscription on the front panel of the altar is taken from the missal. The altar was designed and made by an artist of international renown, Imogen Stuart, Dublin.

Features of the rectangular ruin located in the church grounds suggest that it was a medieval mill. The river running alongside flows into nearby Friar's Lough before becoming a tributary of Lough Derg.

Early Christian to Norman

You next travel up through the village and take the first turn right. On the left, a short distance on, are the remains of the church of an Augustinian foundation. Part of it dates from the 1300s, with later renovations. The west doorway and overhead window have a carved female head and floral and animal motifs.

Next stop is the grounds of the Church of Ireland church. Here one goes backwards in time from the early nineteenth-century Protestant church which was built onto the parish's pre-Reformation one. That church is much older than those encountered at Knigh and Kilbarron and has been dated to the tenth or eleventh century. It is located within the enclosure which housed St. Ruadhan's Early Christian monastery, founded circa AD 550.

A finely-executed limestone doorway inserted in the old church has a male head, floral motifs, a representation of the scourge, and a pelican vulning/extracting blood from its breast to feed its young.

At the village end of the graveyard are remains of two eighth-century high crosses. One has decorative panels with discernible figures of horses and dogs on the base and shaft.

If you walk down a short distance in the direction you were driving you will see the remains of the Norman motte. It is beside a small river and lies within the Early Christian enclosure. The Norman colonisation pattern was to throw up a high mound of earth on which a timber dwelling was built. George Cunningham, Roscrea, in his *The Anglo-Norman Advance into the South-West Midlands 1185-1221,* found that of the twenty-four mottes within his area of study, eight were built on Early Christian sites. He quotes documentary evidence that this motte was destroyed in 1208. Its height was approximately 16.5ft (5m) and the summit diameter less than 33ft (10m).

You now return to the main road to Portumna.

Lough Derg is very close to the road at some points though its waters are obscured by sedge and reeds. A fine expanse of lake and hills come into view some short distance past the 'dangerous bridge', or Ballyeiragh Bridge to give it is correct name, under which flows the river met in Lorrha now heading cross-country for Lough Derg.

The boggy, marshy foundation of this stretch of road makes for a bumpy drive. The road was actually cut through bogland and there's an active bog in to the right where turf cutters and savers can be seen in action during the summer months.

Our next landmark is a nice view of the River Shannon itself to the right, and a multiplicity of signs in the green area – Forest Park, Redwood Castle, horse riding and Birr Castle demesne.

Redwood has a fully-restored MacEgan tower house which is open to the public during the summer months. Guided tours are available.

For a few years in the 1860s a railway link ran between a terminal on the Tipperary bank of the river and the town of Birr, some 14 miles (22km) down the road to the right. It was never a commercial success and went into receivership in 1871. In the aftermath creditors are said to have paid themselves with railway line, sleepers and even the terminal buildings!

The name, Ferry Inn, recalls the fact that a ferry was the only means of crossing the river until the first bridge – a timber one – was built at Portumna in 1796. The next bridge upriver is at Banagher, some 11 miles (17.7km) distant by river.

Short of Portumna Bridge is the entrance to Belle Isle House, one-time home of a family of Seagraves of whom Sir Henry O'Neill de Hane Seagrave, a renowned racing motorist, was a member. He won the French Grand Prix in 1924 and established world speed records of 203 and 231 m.p.h. in 1927 and 1929 respectively. He was aged only 34 years when killed on Lake Windermere in 1930 while attempting to establish a new water speed record.

Other residents of Belle Isle were Yelvertons and Wallers. Looking back one can see the remains of a mid-eighteenth-century windmill (right) on the hill above Belle Isle.

Hayes Island is downriver of Portumna Bridge which spans the River Shannon shortly before it expands to form Lough Derg, the largest of its three lakes.

The present bridge was built in 1911. This gateway to the west of Ireland must also cope with river traffic passing underneath. Accordingly, the portion on the Galway side has a timber section which swivels open to allow vessels to pass without having to lower their masts. During peak season it is opened three times every morning and afternoon on weekdays to facilitate such craft (a timetable is displayed on the bridge). Each boat pays a toll of £1.50.

Bream and rudd are the main species of fish caught in the water along here.

Looking downriver from the bridge, Portumna Castle and Forest Park are on the right bank, while on the left are the ruins of Derry Castle (not always visible) in the townland of Lehinch . This is known locally as 'Ireton's Castle' but without any definite evidence that General Ireton, married to Lord Protector Oliver Cromwell's daughter Bridget, ever passed this way. It was built in the mid-1600s by Sir Charles Coote, President of Connaught.

Near the bridge is a terminus for cruiser hire. Customers can go upriver to Belleek on Lower Lough Erne in Co. Fermanagh, Northern Ireland, or down-lake to Killaloe.

Portumna 'where the West begins'

> Across the Shannon, on the Galway side, rests the town of Portumna. Its clean streets and tidy homes, the well-kept stores and shops, the wide-awake and up-to-date methods of the people, the splendid academy, the public hall furnishing excellent amusements ... these indicate what giant steps Ireland has taken toward that prosperity for which she has longed through the centuries and which she so richly deserves.

Rev. Pathe's observations in 1929 are still valid. The modern Portumna (*port omna/the landing spot of the oak*), which has a population of 1,200, now exploits its location on the river with marinas, nature walks, bicycle hire, golf, angling, arts and crafts, a hotel and guesthouses. These amenities are in much demand, and especially during the annual festival in early July.

The town won a national Tourism Award in 1993 for the presentation of its tourism potential and is twinned with Saint Germaine, France.

A community school caters for 600 post primary pupils there is also a co-educational primary school. The former rectory is home to a residential language school (full board or self-catering) where English and several other languages are taught. It is recognised by the Department of Education.

The history of the town is intimately linked to the Norman family of de Burgo/Burke since William (died 1205) acquired lands in the province of Connaught. His descendant, Ulick, was created earl of Clanrickarde in 1543. Successive earls ruled here almost continuously until the 15th earl's death in 1916. By then the break-up of the extensive estate had commenced following the 1901 Land Act. The title passed to a cousin, the Marquess of Sligo, who merged it with his existing one. For the first time in its history the estate passed to a descendant of a female de Burgo – the grandson of Elizabeth, sister of the last earl. That heir, Viscount Lascelles, married the Princess Royal, daughter of King George V, in 1922. A few years later they visited Portumna and the Princess planted a tree inside the first gate. In 1948 Lascelles sold the 1,400 acre estate to the Irish Land Commission.

A short break in de Burgo ownership arose during the Cromwellian era when the then earl, loyal to the Crown, had his Portumna estates confiscated. The new owner was Henry Cromwell, the Lord Protector's youngest son, appointed as Lord Lieutenant of Ireland in 1659. Cromwell junior enjoyed ownership for three years until the restoration of Charles 11 to the English throne saw the de Burgos reinstated.

Burke Legacies

The de Burgo era left the town with three major assets – the ruins of a Dominican Priory, Portumna Castle, and a magnificent forest park. They are approached either by turning left at the Lough Derg Drive sign as you come into the town, or left at the R.C. church at the top of the town – the latter route is recommended as it brings you quickly to the castle gates and T(ourist) I(nformation) O(ffice). For the Priory continue on past the TIO.

The Priory was established in the thirteenth century by the Cistercians but taken over two centuries on by the Dominicans. Like most religious foundations in the United Kingdom, it suffered the fate of suppression under the reign of King Henry VIII and became Crown property. As such it came into the ownership of the de Burgos and the monks returned for a period. They left again during the Cromwellian period, returned as soon as the de Burgos were reinstated, and continued in residence for several years. The penal law of 1697 which decreed that all Catholic clergy must leave the country marked the beginning of the end of their association with Portumna.

Of particular interest here is the magnificent east window in the choir which is a fine example of 'switch line tracery'. The south transept is lit by another fine one. Part of the foundation's cloister and domestic buildings also survive. Patrick Sarsfield, the Jacobite soldier-hero of the 1691 Williamite siege of Limerick, was married here in 1690 to Honora de Burgo, sister of John, 9th earl.

The ruin was taken into the care of the Office of Public Works in 1951 and has been conserved and beautifully presented ever since.

The marina and the commencement of the Forest Park nature trail are a short drive or cycle past the Priory.

Of the 1,400 acres estate acquired in 1948 about 1,000 are under forestry with a felling programme already in operation. The Forest Park's extensive lakeshore area has a wildfowl sanctuary with observation point, small herds of fallow deer and red deer, and friendly mallard ducks. As well as the pedestrian entrance near the marina, there is an entrance for cars and bicycles a short distance from the town on the Scarriff road.

The entrance to the castle is through the gate opposite the Tourist Information Office.

Castle Re-Opened

1996 marked a watershed in the castle's return to life. Following years of restoration by the Office of Public Works its great hall was opened to the public for the first time. Display panels carry information on the layout of the house and gardens, the restoration work, and a de Burgo/Burke genealogy from the seventeenth-century.

Built at a cost of £10,000 in the early 1600s during the lifetime of Richard, 4th earl, it is essentially a country house with defensive features brought forward from the earlier castles and tower houses. These include machicolation, musket holes, and flanking towers. It stands three stories over a basement and has large rooms lit by regularly-placed windows and commands a fine view of Lough Derg. It was accidentally destroyed by fire in 1826 and remained a ruin thereafter.

The building is approached through three distinctive gates and gardens – all fully restored. The original gardens were the first Renaissance gardens in Ireland – similar to Damer's House, Chelsea, London (1622). The second gate is the reception area.

Portumna is a bustling town whose local population is boosted annually by boat enthusiasts and foreign students. Its two churches are at the far end of the main street. The Church of Ireland church, which was built in 1830 in revival Gothic style, has undergone considerable conservation work and renovation in recent years.

The Catholic church dates only from 1961 and has a separate bell tower.

Back by Borrisokane

As you return from Portumna retrace your drive or cycle as far as Ballinderry then turn left at the garage on the Terryglass side for the 4.5 miles (7.2km) trip to Borrisokane, the capital town of Lower Ormond barony.

On your way you will see remains of a nineteenth-century innovative combination of national school and agricultural school called Kyle Park which is still an attractive though dilapidated two-storey building on the left; the entrances to Kyle Park and Arran Hill Big Houses (both gone); and Tombricane tower house. The latter's date of erection has not been positively determined but its builder was most likely an O'Kennedy – they are returned as occupiers of the area before and after the Cromwellian confiscations of the mid-1600s.

At the bridge in Borrisokane fingerposts point to Portumna (left) and the Old Church Centre straight ahead. The centre, which has a tourism bureau for the area, workspaces and a display area, is the headquarters of Tipperary

Lakeside Co-operative which was established in 1993.

The building (1832) was the parish's R.C. church until a new one was erected at the upper end of the town in 1973. Local effort played a large part in having this fine building preserved and rehabilitated to serve the community in a most useful way. A tablet affixed to an external wall, around to your left, tells an extraordinary story.

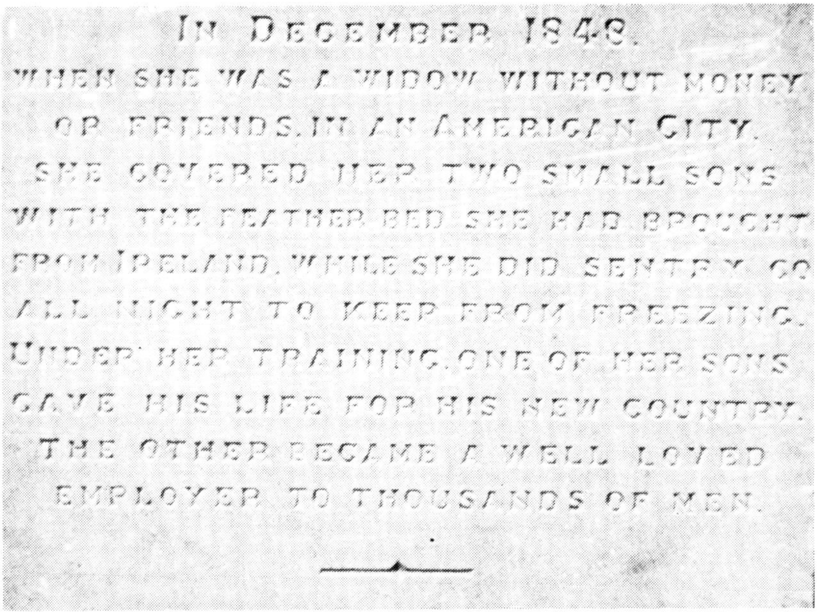

A montage of local lore and genealogical information suggests the following as the *probable* background. Thomas Gleeson of the Silvermines parish, south of Nenagh, married Mary Cleary of Drumnamahane in Borrisokane parish. They decided to emigrate to Canada. He went ahead, but died of yellow fever, as so many did, and is buried on an island in the St. Lawrence estuary. The widow decided to go the USA with her two sons and their few belongings. One of the sons died, in the American Civil War it is believed. One was 'a mechanical genius' and became 'the Ballbearings King of the USA'. This may now be the 'Gleson Works' in Rochester, New York.

Opposite the signposts is one of the finest mills remaining in North Tipperary. It was powered by the Ballyfinboy river and has its wheels and fittings intact. It has been in Heenan ownership since the mid-1920s and ceased operating in 1944.

Borrisokane, which has a population of 784, has a primary school and a post-primary Community College, formerly termed Vocational School and founded in 1942. The college occupies part of Borrisokane Union workhouse.

The name Buirghíos Ui Chéin/Borrisokane stems from the amalgamation of the Norman word burgage, indicating a centre of settlement, and the name Clan Cian or Cianacht a name for the Irish sept of the O'Carrolls. *A Parish History of Borrisokane* (1994), compiled by Eamon Slevin for the local historical society, has details on the town generally, on incidents, personalities, and buildings.

A leaflet compiled and published by the local historical society has brief biographical notes on the town's mill; Methodist Chapel (1811); Church of Ireland church (1812); Convent of Mercy (1887); and the former Rectory (1812) where young Reginald Hitchcock lived for a few years before his father was promoted to Rector of Kinnitty. From there Reginald went to the United States, changed his name to that of his mother's, and as Rex Ingram went on to become a legend in the silent film industry.

Borrisokane can also lay some claim to a modern screen actor in the person of Martin Sheen whose Phelan mother was born in the town. He is a regular visitor to this area.

The Rectory and another building of architectural interest, the Clarke Memorial Hall, are in the vicinity of the Old Church Centre. Harriett Clarke (died 1906) made a bequest to Borrisokane which was used to erect the hall. Her father was David Clarke, Macclesfield, Cheshire, England, who bought the town in 1852 as part of a estate of 1,668 acres when its owner, Thomas Towers, became encumbered with debts. Clarke was Mayor of Macclesfield on one of his visits, in 1868. A memorial tablet in England records his addresses as Macclesfield and Borrisokane.

The Church of Ireland church and the R.C. church are at the Nenagh end of the town. Their foundation dates are one hundred and eighty years apart. The interdenominational graveyard by the 1812 C. of I. church, and the eight memorials within the church, – six of the eight commemorate members of the Stoney family – are most valuable records for local history researchers.

There are ten Kennedy gravestones with dates ranging from 1720 to 1841 and fifteen O'Meara/Mara/Meara ones ranging from 1753 to 1975. Obviously the early ones pre-date the 1812 church. The oldest Kennedy stone is to Darby Kennedy who died in 1720, aged 70 years, which places his birth a few years before the massive expropriation of the lands of the O'Kennedy lords.

In 1974 the remains of four priests of the parish were transferred from the redundant R.C. church to a plot beside the new one. So were those of Very Rev. William Flannery (1830-1901), D.D., Dean of Windsor, Ontario, who had ministered for over forty years on the Canadian missions, notably in the parishes of Amhertsburg and St. Thomas.

He was a renowned fundraiser for new churches and schools, a skill first identified when, as a young curate in Toomevara near Nenagh, he was sent to the USA to collect funds for a projected cathedral in Nenagh. The American

Civil War interrupted that mission, but the funds collected were used by the Bishop of Killaloe to conserve Nenagh Castle by constructing the present upper twenty feet.

Dean Flannery edited and contributed to two Catholic journals – the *Catholic Record* (London, Ontario) and *Catholic Register* (Toronto). He also wrote verse including 'My Coat of Frieze'. The coat had been sent to him by his Nenagh friends. He wrote the words to the traditional Irish air, 'Follow Me Down to Carlow', which had been the principal refrain by a fiddler at a party in a log hut in the backwoods of the priest's mission field.

My Canadian friends, when the Autumn ends
May purchase furs from Hudson Bay,
And Scotsmen bold in the biting cold
Draw close their plaids in blue and grey;
'Mid the howling blast, when the snow falls fast,
How chill their looks and dreary,
While snug and warm I brave the storm
In frieze of Tipperary.

Dean Flannery returned to Ireland in 1901 for health reasons and died a few months later at the home of his sister Julia Delaney here in Borrisokane.

Ardcroney

The next settlement is Ardcroney, 5 miles (8km) on. The R.C. church, was built in 1838 and renovated in 1978 when the bell tower, in round tower style, was added. In the grounds is a mass rock which was brought from the townland of nearby Ballinamurragh. Mass rocks belong to the 1700s when penal laws prohibiting Catholic public worship were in force.

The ruin in the nearby graveyard is that of a church and fifteenth-century castle, both belonging to the medieval Bishop of Killaloe. Later owners were O'Hogans. One also finds members of this sept as tenants of church lands in other areas of North Tipperary.

In recent years a number of pre-historic graves have been identified in the Ardcroney area. The discovery of the first one in 1977 caused considerable excitement. A preliminary excavation by a National Museum of Ireland archaeologist found skeletons of two males and a sherd of pottery. The grave consists of a cist or box-like structure covered by a large cairn of stones. Archaeologists have dated it to circa 2000 BC. It is located on private land a short distance down the road opposite the church.

One of the treasures in the National Museum, Dublin, is the seventh century Ardcroney gold collar. This was found in the area sometime in the nineteenth century – reputedly in a field between the cist grave and the main road.

Another feature in Ardcroney is a turlough or lake which appears and disappears, depending on the level of the water table. Located a few fields from the main road opposite the church, it becomes a resort for swans as soon as the water appears.

National Monument

Another cist grave, which is a national monument, lies in the townland of Ashley Park and has been dated to circa 3000-2500 BC.

To visit this turn right on the Nenagh side of the next garage and agricultural machinery depot, then left again (by the pump) about a half-mile down the bye-road. The grave, with a passage leading into it, covered by a large cairn of stones, and surrounded by two earthen banks, was excavated by the Office of Public Works in 1980.

Human bones and sherds of pottery were recovered in the excavation. The human bones belonged to an adult male, and two children aged six years and one and a half years approximately.

The combination of three features make the monument unusual – its size, 'not quite as big as Newgrange, Knowth or Dowth in the Boyne Valley, but not very far off', the surrounding earthen banks, and the passage feature.

A fine gateway (the same design as that seen at Peterfield/Johnstown, Puckane) marks the entrance to Ashley Park House (now a guesthouse). This eighteenth-century residence, built by John Head is further enhanced by Loughourna Lake in the foreground.

It is 3 miles/5km from here to Scott's Bridge where you turned off for Puckane on the outward journey. On the way there's a nice view of Nenagh set against a backdrop of the Silvermines hills and Keeper Hill.

Index

Aglishcloghane 77
Annagh 64, 67, 68
Annagh Lough 64
Ardgregane 14
Ardnacrusha 39
Ashe Road (Nenagh) 6
Ashgrove Meadows 37

Ballina 6, 33, 37, 38, 39
Ballinderry 70, 71, 72
Ballingeer 28
Ballyanny 57
Ballyanny Upper 56
Ballycaridoge 22
Ballycolliton 63, 66
Ballycolliton river 63, 64
Ballycommon 11
Ballycormac 77
Ballyeiragh bridge 78
Ballyfinboy river 70
Ballymoylan 21
Ballyscanlon 69
Banba/Courthouse Square (Nenagh) 4, 5
Bangor (Nth Wales) 31
Barrack/Kenyon St (Nenagh) 7
Beaumaris (Nth Wales) 31
Belle Isle 79
Belleen Upper 14
Bellevue 68
Birdhill 37
Black Lough 30
Blackfort/Lisduff 60
Brocka 67
Brookfield 69
Brookwatson 55

Cameron Island 64, 65
Carrigahorig 76
Carty's Cross 55
Castle Cambie 66
Castle/Pearse St (Nenagh) 6, 53
Castlelough 31
Castlelough House 33
Castlelough Lakeside Park 29
Castlelough Woods 32
Castletown 29, 31, 32, 35, 40
Castletown (Coolbawn) 66, 68
Castletownarra 22
Castletownarra/Portroe parish 22
Ceann Coraidh/ Kincora 49
Chapel Lane (Ballina) 37
Charley's Hill 28
Clancy's Bridge 34, 36
Clanrickarde estate 80
Claree 63
Claree Lake 63
Clareen Lough 63
Clareen River 14, 15
Clarianna Bridge 56
Clonamuck 11
Cloneygowney 22
Clontarf (Co. Dublin) 49
Clover Hill 14
Coolbawn 65
Coolbawn Cross 67, 68
Cormack Drive (Nenagh) 8
Coumbeg 22
Crannagh 14, 58
Cregane 14
Cuckoo's well 56
Cudville Green (Nenagh) 6
Cudville Road (Nenagh) 6
Curraghbally 31
Curraghbawn 18
Curraghmore 68

Derry Castle/tower house 36
Derry Demesne 34
Derrybeg 34
Derrycastle 34, 36
Drominagh 71
Drominagh Bridge 70
Dromineer 11, 13, 17
Dromineer Castle 13
Duharra 22

Eochaile Ara/Youghalarra 20
Esker Line 15

Fatheen 14
Ferry Inn 79
Firmount 76
Four Roads cross 7
Friar's Island 50
Friar's Lough 78

Garrykennedy 17, 23, 24
Garrykennedy Quay 24
Garrykennedy Wood 24
Garrymacteige 27
Glasshouse, Shinrone 34
Glenbower 65
Gort na Bhfia/Gortnaveigh 18, 20
Gorteenakilla 14
Gortlandroe 8, 10, 14
Gortlandroe Industrial Estate 11
Gortmore point 71
Gowran (Co. Kilkenny) 2
Grange Upper 56
Graves of the Leinstermen 29
Gurteen 77
Gurthalougha House 70

Hayes Island 79
Hogan's Pass 14, 15

Illaunmore/Islandmore 65, 68
Inis Cealtra/Holy Island 19 33
'Ireton's Castle' 80
Ivy Grove 37

Johnstown 61

Keeper Hill 65
Kilbarron 66
Kilbarron Church of Ireland church 67
Kilbarron/Skehanagh Quay 65
Kilcoleman 21
Kilgarvan 69
Killaloe 6, 21, 24, 25, 26, 29, 32, 37, 38, 40
Killashallo 7
Killeen 76
Killodiernan 61, 62
Knigh 57, 60, 63, 67
Knigh Cross 58
Knocknacartan 63
Knockshegowna hill 76
Kylenoe 71

Lackamore 22
Lake Windermere 79
Lakeside Park 30
Lansdowne 26, 28
Lehinch 80
Lesserragh 68
Limerick Road (Nenagh) 54
Lisduff 60
Lisquillibeen 67
Lodge 61
Lookout 33
Lorrha 77
Lough Derg 6, 39, 63, 78, 79
Lough Derg (flora) 64
Lough Derg Way 19, 30
Loughtea Hill 28, 64, 65
Loughtea House 34
Luska 63, 68
Luska House 65
MacDonagh Park (Nenagh) 10
Michael Range 36
Moanree 8
Monroe 18, 21
Mota 69
Mountshannon 33
Muileann O h-Ogain 14
Mungo Park 68
'Mungo Park' 68

Nenagh 1, 3, 29, 51
Nenagh river 2, 54, 55, 56
New Line (Nenagh) 54
Newtown 14, 15, 18, 26
Newtown River 16

Old Court Castle 74
Old Turnpike Road (Nenagh) 54
Ollatrim river 54
O'Meara's Acres 68

Ormond St (Nenagh) 54
Pallasbeg 18
Pallasmore 21
Parteen House 36
Parteen Villa 39
Peter/Kickham St (Nenagh) 53
Peterfield 61
Portroe 15, 23, 26, 27, 30, 36
Portumna 24, 80, 81
Portumna Bridge 79
Portumna Castle 80
Portumna Forest Park 80, 81
Portumna Priory 81
Poulawee 62, 63
Puckane 60, 61

Redwood 79
Richmond Row (Nenagh) 6
River Shannon 26, 32, 34, 35, 36, 37, 39, 49, 79
Rockvalley 61
Ryninch 36

Sallygrove (Nenagh) 54
Scarriff Bay 33
Scilly islands 33
Scott's Bridge 55
Scriboge 69
Skehanagh 65
Slevoir Bay 76
Slieve Aughty 65
Slieve Bernagh 33, 65
Slieve Bloom mountains 76
Solsboro 11

St. Augh's Well 74
St. Conlan/Coonlin's Well 19
St. Conlan's Road (Nenagh) 9
St. Flannan's Cathedral 40, 49
St. Flannan's Oratory 40
St. Flannan's RC church 50
St. Flannan's Street (Nenagh) 52
St. John's Well (Nenagh) 55
St. Joseph's Park (Nenagh) 9, 51, 52
St. Lua's Oratory 50
Stoney High (Nenagh) 14
Summerhill (Nenagh) 9, 53

Templeachally graveyard 39
Templeachally/Ballina parish 34, 37
Terryglass 71, 73, 75
Terryglass church 75
Terryglass Quay 74
Tinarana 34
Tinarana House 35
Tipperary (NR) Co. Council 6
Tonnerre (France) 3
Tountinna Hill 28, 30, 34, 65, 65
Townlough Upper 34
Tuamgraney 33
Tullamore 14
Tyone (Nenagh) 2

Water mill, Newtown 17
White Walls (Nenagh) 9
White Walls Road (Nenagh) 8, 9

Youghal Bay 14, 19, 23
Youghal Quay 18, 22
Youghalarra 7, 15, 18, 21, 27
Youghalarra parish 20, 22
Youghalarra Quay 19
Youghalarra River 22

Tiobraid Árann Ag Faire

At 10.30 a.m. on 19 March 1996 the Greenpeace barge *Bradán Feasa* docked in the shadow of the old castle at Dromineer. All day long students from primary and second level schools all over North Tipperary visited Dromineer. Following an introductory talk by Iva Pocock author of the Greenpeace report 'A Vision for the Shannon's Future', a video was shown. After this introduction to the aims and activities of Greenpeace it was down the stairway to the lower part of the eighty-five foot barge. There the students viewed a very interesting scientific exhibition. They had the chance to discuss the issues of water pollution with Dr David Santillo from the Greenpeace laboratory at Exeter University. After a quick photo-opportunity on the stern deck the students returned to shore to begin the second part of their visit to Dromineer.

The different groups were taken on the 'Dromineer Bay Trail'. The trail concentrates on the historic, scientific and tourism/leisure aspects of Dromineer. It aims to give the students a better picture of the lakeside village and how it fits into the Shannon as a whole. The development of this project was carried out by the post-primary group of Tiobraid Árann ag Faire.

Environmental Awareness

Tiobraid Árann ag Faire (TÁF) is a North Tipperary Vocational Education Committee (VEC) initiative which was set up in 1991 in order to promote environmental awareness in the educational system and among the general public and to develop a model for action which can be replicated elsewhere in Ireland and the European Union.

The Environmental Programme has a core committee of twenty-five persons. The committee is made up of representatives from the primary, post-primary and adult education teaching sectors, National Parks and Wildlife Service, An Taisce, Greenpeace, The Irish Wildbird Conservancy, Tipperary (N.R.) County Council, and the farming community. The working party has a part-time environmental Education Officer and a part-time Community Officer. These, along with the VEC Chief Executive Officer, Lúcás Ó Muircheartaigh, co-ordinate the programme.

Water & Hedgerows

TÁF's post-primary group decided to focus on Transition Year students, and chose as their theme 'Water, A Natural Resource'.

The pack contains four sections focusing on Geography (tourism and environmental issues), History and Science. The final section contains teachers' notes and supplementary material. The pack uses Lough Derg as its main focus; the 'Dromineer Bay Trail' can be carried out by students and follow-up projects completed on returning to class.

The Hedgerow Education Pack for primary schools is intended primarily as a teacher's pack with background information on various aspects of the hedgerow. The pack also includes work cards for use by the students in the field and suggestions for follow-up work and experiments which can be carried out in the classroom.

An important part of the package is its cross-curricular approach to the study of the hedgerow. Suggestions are detailed for poetry, literature, songs, drama, art and crafts, and science and technology, which are related to the theme.

Woodland & Peatland

TÁF leased 6.5 hectares of woodland from Coillte. The wood is part of Doonane Woodlands, about 4 miles from Newport in the Slieve Felim area.

This particular area was chosen because it fulfilled all the requirements felt necessary to educate students and the public in general on the natural history of woodlands: there is a good mixture of broad leaf and coniferous trees, an abundant and diverse ground flora, access to a river, a large open area which can be improved and managed to the benefit of wildlife and it has good accessibiity – an important consideration for the disabled and elderly.

TÁF organises a series of environmental workshops. The first of these was held on 27 April 1996 in Newport. The course was run in conjunction with the Irish Peatland Conservation Council. The workshop's theme was the conservation of Irish peatlands and the use of this valuable natural habitat as a useful teaching tool across the curriculum.

The work of Tiobraid Árann ag Faire gives long-term promise of preservation and enhancement of several aspects of the Lakeside and hinterland environment – of benefit to residents and tourists alike.

Caomhnaigh ár dtimpeallacht
Preserve our environment

Ná loit an todhchaí dár bpáistí!
Do not spoil the future for our children!

Tiobraid Árann ag Faire operates from Ionad Oideachais Ciamálta, Tulach Sheasta (061-378021) and Tipperary (N.R.) VEC offices (067-31250).

Hospitality, History, Happenings
– Marketing Tipperary Lakeside

Local tourism product providers took the initiative to facilitate change and in January of this year Tipperary Lakeside Tourism Co-operative Society was established to promote tourism in the area. Its membership has reached 75 and includes a wide range of businesses engaged in accommodation, leisure activities and services which wholly or partly depend on tourism. The Co-op's marketing plan will complement the promotional efforts of Shannon Development and Bord Fáilte at regional and national level.

The Co-op will be promoting Tipperary Lakeside as a tourist destination offering a variety of activities. Included are walking, cycling, horse-riding, water sport, golf, heritage, nature appreciation and others.
– Michael Lowry, Minister for Transport, Energy, and Communications on the occasion of the official launch of Tipperary Lakeside Tourism Co-operative Society Ltd on 20 October 1995 at Dromineer Bay Hotel.

The Co-op is based at the Old Church, Borrisokane (067-27155), which also provides visitor amenities and a Tourist Information Point, with the support and financial assistance of Shannon Development and FÁS.

... your famed hospitality, and the sense of connectedness it gives visitors. It is the hello on the street, the friendly interest shown even by strangers, the feeling that I am receiving 'a hundred thousand welcomes'. And of course what accompanies the warmth and friendliness in the abiding love of a good story, an involved joke, a bitter-sweet song.

Maybe you have to be from a country which usually dates its history from 1620 to appreciate the fact that here in Ireland you have a very rich lode of recognisable historic events dating back to several thousand years BC. In the lake region, and in fact thoughout the Shannon waterways, I found an amazing number of cultural, natural and literary layers of the past.

Let me tell you about a couple of happenings. I was fortunate to visit during St. Patrick's Day weekend, which coincided with the President's visit to Nenagh. Children, parents, and grandparents massed in the street to greet her in front of the Nenagh Credit Union. I could tell by the smiles on their faces how proud they were to receive Mrs. Robinson, who herself had very happy childhood memories of visits to Nenagh. I felt honoured to be a witness to such an important event and to be introduced to the President at the Heritage Centre.
***– Marguerite Jordan, writing for* Outbound Traveller *magazine, reaching 200,000 US travel agents. She also writes for* The Boston Globe.**